HF442037

Punk Para-Normal Archaeology: Beyond the Hunt and the Archaeological

JOHN SABOL

Copyright 2020 by John G. Sabol and Ghost Excavation Books, Inc., Bedford, PA, USA. All rights reserved.

Front cover and back cover design by Mary Becker. Front cover photo: Ruins, c. unknown, historical archival photo, Kindle Books. Back cover photo: John Sabol, Lobby Area, Omni Bedford Springs Resort & Spa, USA.

The right of John G. Sabol to be identified as the author of the text concepts has been asserted in accordance with section 77 and 78 of the Copyright, Design & Patent Act 1988.

<u>Warning</u>, the text herein is fully protected by U.S. Federal copyright laws. Federal copyright laws will be vigorously enforced and infringement will be prosecuted to the fullest extent of the law, which can include damages and lawyer's fees to be paid by the infringer of copyright. No part of this book may be reproduced or transmitted in any form or by any means, electronic or mechanical, including photocopying, recording or by any information storage and retrieval system without written permission from the publisher. For additional copyright information contact Ghost Excavation Books, Inc., at ghost.excavation@yahoo.com.

Photo credits: Historical archival photos. All other photos, names, and original photos are used with permission and copyrighted by their respective owners

Copyright © 2020 John G. Sabol

All rights reserved.

ISBN: 9798638978525

Ghost Excavation Books, Inc.™©
A division of I.P.E. Research Center™©,
Bedford, PA, USA
www.ghostexcavation.com

OTHER BOOKS BY JOHN G. SABOL

Also by John Sabol...
Ghost Excavator (2007)
Ghost Culture (2007)
Gettysburg Unearthed (2007)
Battlefield Hauntscape (2008)
The Anthracite Coal Region (2008)
The Politics of Presence (2008)
Bodies of Substance, Fragments of Memory (2009)
Phantom Gettysburg (2009)
Digging Deep (2009)
The Re-Haunting(s) of Gettysburg (2010)
The Haunted Theatre (2011)
Ghost Culture Too (2012)
Beyond the Paranormal (2012)
Digging-Up Ghosts (2nd publishing, 2013)
Burnside Bridge (2013)
The Gettysburg Experience (2013)
The Absence Above, A Presence Below (2013)
The Production of Haunted Space (2013)
Centralia, Pennsylvania (2013)
The Ghost Excavation (2013)
The Good Death and the Civil War (2014)
Centralia: A Vision of Ruin (2014)
Altered States: Making the Extraordinary
Ordinary Again (2014)
Archaeology and Ghost Research: A Relational Entanglement (2014)
Performances in Haunted Space: An Afterlife in Ruin (2014)
Haunting Presences, Ruins, and Ghostly Entanglements (2015)
The Afterlife of Centralia: Presences in a Landscape of
Destruction (2015)
An Archaeology Without Borders: Performance Excavations in
Embedded/Entangled Fields (2016)

Ghost Excavator Books, Inc. ™ ©

Bedford, Pennsylvania,
USA

CONTENTS

PREFACE: A NEW 'NORMAL'?

"We are in the midst of crisis, which means that it is precisely not limited to the crisis of knowledge, but that we are – in some sense – in the *presence* of crisis"

• Theodor Barth (2019).

I am writing this amid the pandemic of the coronavirus onslaught. The virus, and its social and economic effects, besides the medical, serves as an important baseline to compare with less serious endeavors. In the modern world, but not restricted to it, we seek new knowledge about old things and processes. One is this eruption of a new virus spreading throughout the world. Yet, such viruses are as old as 'mankind' (or 'people kind') itself. In this pursuit of knowledge, we seek to eradicate its consequences by demanding immediate results beneficial to all.

We, however, do have immediate results that have affected almost everyone: the disruption of the social gathering, including the academic as the pursuit of knowledge, apart from the immediate medical emergency. We no longer (for how long nobody knows) can gather together in groups to learn, to entertain, to watch 'live' sports or a play, to eat out in restaurants and drink socially. This hits hard for many, but a lesson we must follow, a plan we must endure, for the benefit of all.

On a less (considerably less) plane of sociable entertaining gathering is the 'ghost hunt', dark tourism, and para-conference venues. No longer should we merely 'entertain' the idea of mere entertainment at/in certain places, seeking acts of translation between past and present, between those that are gone, and those that survive, and this includes archaeological fieldwork. Perhaps ethnographic fieldwork in other places and other cultures is over, at least for the time being.

The work of what happened in these places in the past, and what is happening today in cultures all around the world, excavations and ethnographies, will remain, for the time being, unfinished business. Foremost of these, as considerably less significant, is the weekend excursions to haunted sites. So, as I write this, and for those who read this, let's learn the 'ruin' lesson: let's be serious and empathetic when our fieldwork begins again.

Is the return of a 'revenant' (a 'ghost') repeating itself in the return of a new (but old) type of destruction, this pandemic of 2020? Here, in the United States, is it the return of the 'unnamed' dead, a similarity to the 'ghosts' of the flu virus of 1918? For thousands upon thousands of years, we have seen these 'unnamed' dead, the crisis of epidemics, both regional and global. How many billions of individuals have gone unnamed through history, throughout prehistory. What, then, is the sometimes urgency in today's world to identify these 'ghosts', these 'unnamed' dead, especially now in the midst of this pandemic, one that may be a recurring, returning 'revenant' that will 'haunt' future generations?

The question, in this current writing you are reading now, is this: Is ghost hunting, as a focus on the present, as it is practiced today, (in behaviors, in status seeking, the use of contemporary technologies, the questions to empty space) morally wrong, or now irrelevant? Is it a symptom of excessive, troubled (and restless) egos? What has worried me for some time is the heightened interest among ghost hunters in the 'ruin porn', frequent investigations amid ruin, in buildings of various stages of ruination, and in abandoned landscapes, as a form of 'ruin paranormal'. What viruses and other deadly bacteria may remain embedded in these locations, attached to the material culture that remains? Maybe, ghost hunters should follow the lead of archaeologists, who wear protective masks and gear when they explore tombs and other 'underground' remains?

These ruins and abandoned buildings, so popular with ghost hunters, do have an 'afterlife', if 'afterlife' is defined as "the range of life [that] must be determined by history, rather than by nature" (Benjamin 1968:71). That history must be explored, but as the 'para-history' of ghost hunters? Relevancy and context, now more important than ever, lies not in a 'hunt' but in serious fieldwork, the acquisition of meaning-making knowledge production.

Julie Cruikshank (2005), in working with indigenous peoples in the Yukon, has said her informants believe that glaciers can 'listen'. These glaciers, they say, respond to human behavior. Crisca Bierwert (1999), in her ethnographic work among the Coast Salish of British Columbia and Washington State has said this:

"The concept of place…can imply binary complementarities, like provider and receiver…those who frequent a place become part of one another's ambiance of that place" (1999:44).

What effects do contemporary ghost hunting have on the local environment, especially if there is still 'attached' presence there, amid the ruin and abandonment? If we conceive of haunted sites as a 'host' ('provider') environment, what do ghost hunters bring (especially at paranormal 'hot spots') to these locations in the context of huge public ghost hunt 'edutainment', and recurring ghost tourism? Do these contemporary 'ghosts' create, by bringing different experiences and memories to the 'host' site, more social and physical ruination at these locations?

As Coll Thrush (2011) has stated: "places are sentient and have historical agency in their own right, affirmed by generations of embodied human experience" (2011: 55). Ghost hunting, as 'entertainment' in many of these 'hunts', destroys that 'host' ('provider') relationality, the assemblage of space, humans, environment, objects, experiences, memories, and ghosts, as these sites (even in a state of abandonment and ruin) become 'receivers' of different effects from scores of ghost hunts that evolve into large entertainment venues. These public 'hunts' destroy the social and cultural symmetry of places, perhaps even inscribing other cultural 'footprints' for those 'unnamed' dead.

There is a lot of talk today about 'social distancing' in this current pandemic crisis. The idea of a haunting is 'social distancing' for many. They stay far away from it. For others, like ghost hunters, social distancing is created in fieldwork at these haunted locations. This happens when ghost hunters use non-context-specific behaviors and the use of unknown technologies in an attempt to document ghostly presence, a flawed exercise to (re)-unite two worlds, one past and present and the other contemporary, that had become incompatible at the moment of death, or at the time the location became abandoned.

Perhaps, open public ghosts hunts in the future should be curtailed at paranormal 'hot spots', as a remembrance of what has happened today in the world. And when investigating potential (perceived) haunted locations, should ghost hunters maintain not only social distance, but also refrain from their 'normal' form of 'cultural distancing', as they explore the various layers of memory at these sites?

In this era of a viral pandemic, let's re-consider the 'ghost hunt' as a form of 'edutainment'. Let's also consider the possible effects of the increasing use of ghost tech devices and other technological devices that are used on these 'hunts': "things that have once been in contact remain united" (Taussig 1993: 47-57):

"Might the touch, the sweat,…even a laborer or a user at some distance- remain as residue, even immaterial gestural residue, of/as the device itself?" (Schneider 2019: 56). What about the materials from other lands used in these devices, the work flows and movements of other cultural realms that manufacture these devices? What effects do they retain within the technologies used in contemporary ghost hunting?

"If we think about the intra-in-animation of media in the lives not only of miners, factory workers, retailers, and other laborers but also of consumers or operators or even passers-by who engage with media devices…is it possible to think of those bodies, too, as components" (Ibid: 56) in the spread of viruses? Is this entanglement a "kind of geologic remain" (Schneider 2019: 57). Is it also a kind of 'ghost', extending a 'haunting' to a different form of 'materialization', one that may create a 'pandemic effect'? Are 'ghost tech' devices already 'haunted' objects because of their processing, manufacturing, and distribution from other times and places to the current site of a 'ghost hunt'?

This process of 'ghostly' entanglement "starts with the *encounter* of a human actor with a thing [the ghost tech device]. In the first moment of encounter, humans do not trigger a change in the thing, but the thing changes humans. Merely, its material presence changes perceptions of social space and of movements, and forces humans to modify their social practices" (Stockhammer 2020:36; cf. Gibson 1986).

Ghost hunters must also become aware of "possible toxic legacies of [this] technological culture" (Parikka 2019), which through ghost tech devices, can spread both spatially and temporally as contamination at paranormal 'hot spots'. This occurs through the various exchanges and movements of these devices from raw material to product to use at haunted locations. How is this transference and transformation affecting both the ghost hunter, the 'ghost hunt' and the haunted site?

What about the residue of "zombie media"?

"If the objects of old media are abandoned…what becomes of the bodily habits those once-new objects congealed in the bodies of users? Where have they gone?…Is there a mode of remaining in…the role of the hand…a handheld object or an object passed hand to hand"? (Schneider 2019: 81).

There is something to think about regarding the (extensive) use these 'things' (the ghost tech device) in the hands of ghost hunters, especially during a public ghost hunt when scores of people are moving around with these devices in sometimes enclosed spaces. Today, the world is full of these 'other', non-human (never human) 'ghosts'. We don't need to populate these places with 'demons', or call some of these haunted sites 'portals to hell'.

Finally,

"acknowledging ghosts is acknowledging and caring for the dead…it is an action of cultural survival" (Jill C. Grady 2011: 293-94).

In this time of a pandemic, both human and cultural survival is important to all of us, as are our 'ghosts'! The goal of this book is to identify a new 'normal' paranormal, one which helps to maintain these haunted places as sites of continuity and memory and, perhaps, in the future, as important locations of particular intangible cultural heritage.

To consider the reality of ghosts (as more than material remains of the past in the present) and spirits (as ancestors) challenges scientific thinking to "tidily organize our messy being into sealed and arbitrary divide between what is sensed (and recorded) as real and what is not. Yet this sense of 'other' is quite natural for most non-Western cultures.

Do these saturations of contemporary presence centered around paranormal 'hotspots', the proliferation of ghost hunting groups, and the continuing increase of 'dark tourism' as ghost tourism, have presence and performance effects on underlying social strata beyond these locations? Do they affect geo-environmental processes there, seasonal cycles, and ecosystem equilibrium that can create a different form of 'haunting'? Do these presence/performance effects 'affect' other than the world of the paranormal in general, and ghost hunting in particular? Does ghost tech saturation at these sites, as a form of "vibrant matter" (Bennett 2010), exert influence upon more than the surrounding physicality of these sites?

As the 'hunt' for ghosts continues after the pandemic 'lockdown', and contemporary presences begin to gather anew at haunted locations, passively recording a form of both material and sensory traces left behind, the question becomes what will this renewed sociality, and its residue mean for future generations of non-ghost hunters? Will these sites merely become a form of 'residue waste' that continues to grow, or something else?

It takes time to 'dig deep' into a potential haunting: no weekend jaunt to one site and then another. It's easy to take surface scans with electronic devices, ask questions to darkened, empty spaces, monitor a site from remote locations, waiting for something 'uncanny' to happen. But there is another 'reality' to meaning, and a 'meaningful' investigation at haunted locations.

It's about getting the 'haunter' identified (and that includes accepting, you the ghost hunter, as that 'haunter'). It's getting history less wrong, by going beyond the 'para-history'. It's acknowledging that the process of investigation (and identifying 'other' normal processes of becoming present) is more meaningful than any manifestation, be it perceived or recorded. The 'dig' site, and its processing, must create a record of a life (an individual or group 'afterlife'), not death. This is achieved through detailed traces, an accurate and ephemeral record of 'sensorial memory' with these past 'taskscapes' of a site's occupational history.

Let's make it quite 'normal' today here in 'Western Culture', as a move away from the 'traditional' ghost hunt and paranormal investigation, a 'normal' movement of empathy and respect at these locations. Let's begin a new phase of investigative work, a new 'normal' for the paranormal.

Bedford, Pennsylvania (USA)
April 2020.

THE 'GHOSTLY' DILEMMA: MASKING THE 'NATURAL' AND 'NORMAL'

If ghosts are real, and are still attached to a world, then that (their) world is not our world today. It is the world of their experiences and memories, habits and knowledge. It is not the changes, both socio-cultural and technological that have occurred since their biological death. The 'unnamed' dead have their own 'named' ghosts. It is contained within today's world of 'ghost hunting'.

The encounters at a site (especially one perceived to be haunted) during fieldwork "is a form of manifestations of the past as culture. It is a cultural encounter…it develops in the triangle of assimilating the resident principles [found locally at the site], negotiation with the institutional framework within which the query is taking place…and the definition of hospitality terms to 3rd parties (past, present, and future)" (Barth 2019: 11).

This is acting in accordance with what occurred at the site (the 'host' site's record of experience and memory). This is negotiated through context-specific performance practices, such that the investigation team is not a 'ghost', bringing something different from past experiences that will affect the future perception of the site. We don't want the 'ghosts' of 'ghost hunters' haunting the 'host' site. We don't want the 'ghosts' to fear the 'unnamed' living who now 'haunt' their sites, the hordes of ghost hunters who are now occupying these 'haunted' sites during a 'hunt'.

The investigation of haunted sites should be an ethnographic, not paranormal, gaze upon that world, and it requires a particular ethno-archaeological, not technological, sensibility and sensitivity to ascertain how material culture, past space (as particular 'taskscapes'), and memory speaks to that other presence that is the 'ghost'. A 'taskscape' is a resonating field of activity in specific spaces at a location. This activity includes phenomena ranging from non-human animals to environmental conditions and processes. A 'taskscape', thus, is a "totality of rhythmic phenomena" (Ingold 1993: 163). At haunted locations, it is not just the 'ghost' that 'haunts'.

These 'tasks', and their coordination, had the effect of drawing the presences of the past into webs of practices, as bundles of rhythms. This becomes a 'meshwork', a multiplicity of lines or paths that weave into each other or diverge (Ingold 2007: 80-81). They can be lines of internal growth, or of persistence through time, as, I propose, in a haunting.

Ghost tech devices, its scanning and measuring 'gaze', nor its use as an object of interpretation, can imaginatively (or ethnographically) 'capture' the reality of this 'meshwork' experience and memory at those haunted sites. Ghost hunting, in its 'hunt' for a scientific approach, forgot that the world is "a multiply animate cosmos wherein no thing is definitively void of expressive agency or life" (Abrams 2018:5). They haven't learned that "all things have agency, the capacity to act. Every phenomenon is potentially animate. Everything moves…" (Ibid: 4). And this certainly includes their ghost tech devices.

Many perceived 'haunted' sites, especially ruins and abandoned buildings, seemingly an absent presence and without known sources of power, do, nevertheless, contain "the affective *properties* or *qualities* exuded by materials, substances, elements, molecules, chemicals, phenomena…felt by sentient beings" (Pauketat 2020: 8). Pauketat (2013: 25) argues that this 'bundle' is a set of distinct things, substances, or qualities wrapped or entangled in unique ways. A 'haunting' is one unique way. This 'bundle' includes the electronic scans and effects of ghost hunting electronic device use as one moves about a location. Fieldwork at these sites must separate those 'qualities' that are the result of these ghost tech scans, the emotional qualities of a 'ghost hunt', those past cultural context experiences learned in particular social settings (the 'taskscapes'), and those properties that are transmitted by memory and still remain embedded/attached in the record of 'presence' of a haunted location.

Ghost hunting must distinguish between the geological, the archaeological, the ethno-historical, the contemporary sociological, and the possible haunting record of a site and their effects on interpretation. Each of these records speak to a different interaction:

- What material cultural remains of the past in the

> present?;
> - What environmental processes continue?;
> - What actions (ethno-historical) still remain attached to the site?;
> - What contemporary social interactions affect perception (the sociology of ghost hunting)?

The entanglement between these records argues that along with important differences, there are significant continuities. This raises questions about the superficial surface probes of contemporary ghost hunting, considering that all pasts exist on the surface, or are capable of surfacing at any time. Ian Hodder (2012) has formulated a "theory of entanglement" to address the complexity and messiness of these relationships between past and contemporary humans, their material culture, and the surrounding physical environment. This could serve as an important baseline for any investigation of potential haunted space.

He argues for a "dialectic of dependence and dependency between human and things". Some of these entangled relationships are enabling. They create dependence. Others are constraining. They limit insights into meaning and interpretation. (cf. Hodder 2012:206). The use of ghost tech devices in ghost hunting is, I propose, both creating dependence (a reliance on these devices by ghost hunters) and dependency (the dependence on these devices creates a narrow view of haunting phenomena, and an inaccurate one. It does not account for these 'other' possible 'normal' hauntings.

Ghost hunters must also consider the concept of the palimpsest: 'sweepings' that erase or suppress past memories and those that 'inscribe'(add to) the record of a haunted location. Both are part of site formation processes. This includes contemporary actions, including technological usage, in ghost hunting (and ghost tourism) activities.

Do haunted sites become 'haunted' by a choreography manipulated by ghost tech devices and a 'script' called 'ghost hunting'? Does it create data praised by audiences of ghost hunters as dramatic and meaningful? Because of the power of social media, does the 'play' of technology remain (to date) a long running theatrical production devoid of meaningful substantive information called 'para-history'? This 'play' may already be in production even before the 'actors' enter onto the 'stage' of a 'ghost hunt'.

A site, including a haunted one, is a "meshwork" (Ingold 2011: 67-75), a web of relationships that is constantly in the process of becoming present. This negates the usual way of seeing a site as a bounded location, and closed off from the rest of external processes. There are lines of movement that weave themselves around the world, thus making them inseparable from the surrounding environment (Ibid: 69). Any investigation of a haunted location must come to grips with its 'meshwork'.

Any assertions, be they archaeological, geological, historical, sociological, or paranormal in nature, impact other humans. This impact is continuous and continues to grow as a 'haunting' (other than 'ghostly') assemblage.

Ghost hunters must proceed with caution. They do have responsibilities. This is because actions, perceptions, do have impact on other parts of the 'reality assemblage' of a site's entangled 'meshwork', including those of the 'ghosts' ghost hunters both seek and create.

There is also the problem if a perceived haunting materialization is understood in relation to a particular segment of time: the contemporaneity of what is now sensed or recorded as manifesting, rather than a relation between various (non-paranormal) entanglements in the 'meshwork' of a site. This is especially important if these entanglements continue through large periods of time. One solution is to abandon the division between past, present, and future as a succession of temporal categories (cf. Lucas 2015: 10-11). Do ghost hunters make, and eliminate, that separation?

Instead, actuality can be taken to be points of contact where a variety of connections and entanglements of different time periods can occur. A relational archaeology (cf. Alberti 2016) considers 'personhood' to also include other-than-human beings, such as animals, plants, spirits, and inanimate things (Fowler 2016). Some of the prominent tropes in this relationality in archaeology include object-based agencies, and their 'biographies (cf. Mills and Walker 2008, among others).

Agency includes "the power of objects to shape human behavior" (Zedeno 2013: 121). I would include ghost tech devices as 'agentic'. The idea of the "meshwork" (Ingold 2011), where relationships, both human and non-human, are in a constant state of flux and movement, is a central concept in this relational archaeology. Objects, such as ghost tech devices, can operate as relational 'beings' independent of humans. Thus, they can 'detect' an event which may be 'perceived' as a haunting but, in reality, may form part of a site's relational component (as non-paranormal process). This ghost tech 'activation' can, in some cases, leave detectable traces, perhaps 'energetic' traces of prior 'ghost hunts', which may 'activate' during future ghost hunts at the site. This 'technological residue', then, may be perceived (or recorded) as 'haunting phenomenon' in this future ghost hunt.

Is a 'haunting', then, a co-equal assemblage (or 'bundle') of both human and non-human (technological and geo-environmental) residue and interactive presence? Do assemblages from different times afford (create) a 'haunting' atmosphere, some percolating and manifesting in the present, while others persist and effect the future?

This 'other' haunting phenomena gathers and folds, affecting in unexpected, uncanny ways at particular points of time in specific spaces and layers of presence within different foldings of time: cyclical, recurring, intermittent, etc. The question is: can this assemblage of time/process/manifestation be recorded in a controlled manner of a site's 'meshwork', without imposing a perception of a paranormal event? We are literally standing on the surface of untold stories, percolating presences, and a 'restless' site record. But, by standing ground, within 'habitual practices as a 'ghost hunt', ghost hunters remain embedded and attached to their paranormal-inspiring practices, without considering 'other' elements of a site's 'bundled' assemblages..

The discipline of archaeology can provide a fertile ground of isolating and separating this 'meshwork' record which can be "read as indices of a variety of relationships, precisely because they 'trouble' the present with objects and substances that have crossed temporal boundaries" (Fredengren 2016: 488). This means that archaeology can "reveal alternative assemblages, arrangements, and relationships" (Ibid: 483) that are not part of the current practices of ghost hunting.

These alternatives rely on an 'otherworldly' rationale, that of the surface 'afterlife' of past and present rhythms and sensory residues. Such an approach can "create the possibility of seeing [and experiencing] *other ways of being in the world*" (Fredengren 2016: 483; emphasis in original). Examples of this archaeological approach can be found below in the sections that follow.

Many times there is an assumption that emotion is a universal construct that can be applied spatially through all haunted sites, and through time there. This universality of emotions is part of popular culture, the 'wargasm' of battlefield reenactments and the success of these costume dramas. It is even promoted as historical fact in television documentaries. But it is not what is occurring at a haunted location. A more ethno-archaeological approach to emotion is needed.

An "archaeology of emotion is a sophisticated, analytical,

and disciplined field, which properly takes emotion to be the subject, rather than the method, of study" (Tarlow 2012:172). Is the "elucidation of human experience…a legitimate and important contribution that archaeology might make" (Ibid: 172)? Can ghost hunters apply this same discipline to fieldwork at haunted locations, instead of the 'normal' edutainment of a 'ghost hunt', especially a public 'ghost hunt'? This can become, I propose, a meaningful form of analyzing what is occurring at these haunted locations

Meaning in fieldwork operations at these haunted locations is a particular situated mode of understanding contexts (both physical and social), and this would include past emotional experience. Without context, there is ample space for ambivalence and indeterminacy in assigning meaning to any perceived 'uncanny' incident or event that may occur. In this regard, the positioned subjectivity of the investigator is important, a point stressed in archaeological fieldwork (cf. Shanks and Tilley 1992). But this 'subjectivity' is "not in itself a methodology for understanding the emotions of past people" (Tarlow 2012: 179) in archaeology, nor at a haunted location today, especially when working in ruin and abandoned buildings at night and in darkness.

Fieldwork must be a 'practicing' of space which makes its past spaces of occupation meaningful. This meaning must be consistent with the past experiences of those who occupied those spaces as specific layers of 'hosts', not 'ghosts', who come to these haunted locations with 'other' experiences, memories, and technologies, such as in the paranormal field.

This other, 'ghostly' presence, such as ghost hunting/paranormal investigation, challenges previous occupational experiences at a site. It creates tension, not communication, between 'host' and 'ghost' (those who are of the site from the past, and those who come to the site in the present), resting upon differences and an opposed POV.

In ghost hunting, as contemporary "ghosts' of presence, there is also the problem between 'haunted' and 'haunting'. The first is an influence from knowing the 'para-history' of a site; the second is being influenced by the visual gaze of the site itself, or by personal memories brought to the site during the investigation. Such contemporary memories produce a 'haunting', even before fieldwork begins. These contemporary memories are 'internal' rather than 'external' ghosts, brought to the site, the production of an individual's character, rather than a literal 'ghost'. Some 'ghost hunts' do carry this 'ghostly' baggage to the site during an investigation.

The question of 'who' is the 'ghost', be it a real past presence or the 'ghost hunter' who brings their contemporary world to the site, centers on a "performative paradox" (Fabian 1991): acts that bring about the 'objectification' of the 'other' ('ghost') – the 'ghost' as object rather than 'subject', be it in the form of a visual anomaly, an EVP, a measured deviation, 'triggering' a ghost tech device, to name a few.

We must expose these modes of presentation on social media, signs of a haunting that reduce it to 'objects' or automatons responsive to technological stimulation. This merely creates entertainment value, not a means of real knowledge production. Ghost hunters still cannot describe its 'subject' of inquiry: a 'real' ghostly presence, a 'dead' human.

Why objectify social spaces once constructed by cultural practices of people who were subjects with identities? This research is not about storytelling, albeit ghost stories. The real 'ghost story' is about communication with possible real past presence, not imagined, technologically-structured, wished for, or invented presences. Otherwise, assumed 'real' knowledge is pure fabrication.

Like theater, performances in haunted spaces should make the investigator experience some emotional trace of the past, and presences who may be attached to those spaces. We can no longer use typologies to classify haunting experiences and box haunted space into a particular ordered way: as a specific type of haunting and/or particular type of manifestation (aided by technology and past para-histories). We cannot take ghosts for granted by fitting them into neat subjective, non-context-specific categories.

We must shift our attention from a concept of representation (a particular ghost as a specific type) to a specific view of an individual, based on a manifesting presence, itself derived from a particular (and known) individual's experiences and knowledge (known up to the time of death). This would take the supernatural quality out of the perception of a particular haunting. A ghost does not learn after death. That idea is 'paranormal'. Huber (2019) asks this relevant question regarding these typologies of ghostly forms: do "different ghosts and spirits themselves…offer different methodologies depending on what a scholar is trying to accomplish" (2019: 17)? She suggests that "how to know ghosts is not to learn how to listen. How to know ghosts is to learn how they listen" (Ibid: 25). Anthropologist Patrice Ladwig (2013) has said this:

"ghosts can be beings with desires, with tastes, with biographies. They appear in specific ways at places at a certain time…and demand a certain treatment as social beings" (2013: 428).

The ruin or abandoned building, a traditional site of ghost hunting, is an historical 'artifact' of both present and contemporary past. But any spectral 'inhabitants' who may remain there lack any attached ability to develop and probably adapt to a contemporary ghost hunting setting, with their new experiences, situations, behaviors, and technologies.

The ghost cannot be 'modernized' because the reason why it remains is it's attachment to past experience and memory, not present day ghost hunting practices and technologies. These contemporary representations will only alienate, I propose, any 'interactive' presence. The ghost's personal history is rigidly bounded, frozen to a particular time. A haunting is a reenactment of that past field of memory, based on those experiences. Either the ghost hunter immerses into that reenactment or else nothing usually occurs.

Finally, if haunted locations are perceived as real 'grave sites' of ghosts, attached to (not interred) a particular earthly space and certain situations, events, or habits, then the construction of these sites as haunted is humanitarian (cf. Laqueur 2015), not edutainment. We must treat these spaces with respect. It's time to be serious about a haunted location. It's time to change the concept of a 'hunt'!

In this book, the strategies of perception and persuasion in documenting a haunting, and haunted site, and the style of fieldwork that constitute and govern the ways of contemporary 'ghost hunting' is discussed. In particular, the means on which data is produced and judgements are made is analyzed.

HAUNTED 'HUNTING', OR 'HUNTING' THE GHOST IN THE 'HAUNTED' MACHINE

Are humans being removed, more and more, from the center of attention of haunting phenomena, being replaced by the 'ghost in the machine'? Jeffrey Sconce, in *Haunted Media* (2000) has said this:

"Where there was once the 'real' there is now only the electronic generation and circulation of almost supernatural simulations. There are now only the ghosts of fragmented, decentered, and increasingly schizophrenic subjectivities. Where there was once meaning, 'history'…there is now only a haunted landscape of vacant and shifting signifiers" (2000: 170-71).

Are these 'shifting signifiers', the 'para-history' of 'ghost hunting', an identification of meaning without substance? Are ghost hunters responsible for this lack of substance, a result of their use of ghost tech devices?

Ghost tech scans, measurements, and 'activations' take ghost hunting into new territory, most of which is not a human cultural haunting (let alone a never-human one). This is because these devices can "reorganize sensory capabilities [cause them to] react to skin and touch, register movement as well as voice…" (Parikka 2012: 20).

This technological "culture presents a new challenge in understanding…the way in which our cognitive and perceptive capabilities are being trained anew in the midst of 'smart environments' that measure, react to and survey us" (Ibid: 21).

Are these ghost hunting tech devices, then, not informing us of real manifestations of a human ghostly presence in the present? Probably. Lucy A. Suchman (2007) has explored this other manifestation that 'haunts' through the idea of agency at the interface between humans and machines.

Is there, then, really something (someone) there in the dark, amid the stillness, occupying empty spaces, besides a ghost hunter's imagination or the 'ghost in the machine'? Has ghost hunting been merely, for all the effort of thousands, a simple exercise in futility or is it still a worthwhile attempt to uncover the hidden dimension of another reality?

Recent years have seen a concerted interest and effort in 'things', readings, and measurements from ghost tech devices and other borrowed technologies, and the non-(never) human that haunt these paranormal locations. Is this post-humanistic turn adversely affecting the way ghosts and haunting phenomena are perceived?

Has ghost hunting/paranormal investigation become more and more a form of 'savage thought' (cf. Levi-Strauss 1966), technological atmospheres that serve as conduits in the perceptual and thinking processes of ghost hunters?

Does this 'savage thought' embody a paranormal that is 'savage' enough to unsettle the human dead from its position as <u>the</u> ghostly presence?

Has 'shadows', changes in environmental conditions, EVP, photographic anomalies, even 'orbs' (for some) become "floating signifiers" that are distributed worldwide through social media, of this now 'normal' paranormal? Has this 'normal' become a solid baseline on which all data should be disseminated and flow out to ghost hunting groups around the world? Are ghost hunters so attached to this 'savage' way of thinking that any deviations from these 'normal' forms of knowledge acquisition and production is considered heretical?

Have these ideas become so engrained in the minds of ghost hunters (and TV producers) that these 'things', readings, measurements ascended above their earthly presence to become non-things, readings, and measurements, becoming the 'ghost' ghost hunters seek? Have they become an engrained index of agency (cf. Miller 1987), as an ongoing paranormal assemblage (cf. Latour 1993) of an 'haunting' event? Ghost hunters have "never been modern", however, with this form of 'technological animism' and their extensive use of technologies!

Such an assemblage has become a pure 'paranormal;' form of a haunting, its 'normal' perception, that is 'read' in a ghost hunt, and exposed on social media. The data taken from their tech devices become 'tags' of paranormal activity, identifying them as objects (not 'subjects' with 'identity') of study and post field analysis. This is casually (not causally) done, with no particular proposal of what they might be 'signifying' in relation to a human presence, including what it being a 'thing', 'measurement', 'reading' of. These 'ghosts in the machine' do not have the "ability to be other to themselves…gain depth, bend, and extend beyond the scope of the actual recordings into scenarios of everyday life" (Espirito-Santo 2019: 10-11).

Yet, these 'signifiers' are based on nothing more that subjective generalizations (no more than un-researched speculation), and usually have little to do with the understanding of space, the sequencing of cultural deposits, site formation processes, and memory fields (to name a few). Why hasn't the everyday in "small things forgotten" become the normal rather than these 'other' becoming paranormal?

These 'small things' that manifest are not so much a 'return' (a 'revenant') as they are a 'perdurance' in place. Ingold (2010) has argued that we "should be interested in 'the persistence of things' rather than 'their antiquity'. This would be important at a haunted location in order to ascertain how a haunting becomes configured in a certain way in relation to what occurred there relative to things, people, spaces, outside forces, and so on.

Yet, the perceived 'otherness' of manifestations is quickly assigned to the margins, the 'dark spaces' of abandoned homes, buildings, and other sites in ruination, where they are allowed more meaning (to the ghost hunter) as presence. In the absence of (observable) people in these locations, the human 'ghost' is replaced by 'things', measurements, and spooky ambiance that 'confirm' its 'haunted' nature.

Ghost hunters conceive of a cause and effect relationship between their ghost tech devices and a manifestation. There may be a relationship, but the same cause (a ghost tech device 'activation') would not have the same effect at different sites and spaces, where other histories (and relational assemblages) in the interaction may differ (perhaps significantly). What we need in a 'haunting' is what Bennett (2010) has described as "emergent causality" (2010: 28): effects are caused by the coming together (emergence) of the different components in an assemblage, characteristic of that's site's biographical record. Thus, "causality is emergent from specific configurations of forces, relations, and entities" (Fowler 2013: 27), and not necessarily 'verified' from a ghost tech device activation alone.

Though there is no right way (as yet) to conduct fieldwork at perceived haunted locations, there are many wrong ways that can affect the perception of the past and its presence in the present. In this book, I consider various implications of these issues, and offer some alternatives to 'normal' ghost hunting/paranormal investigation.

The problem is not simply what people 'normally' read about the paranormal, or view on social media and internet channels and TV programming. There is also the issue of communication: transferring this acquired information into the field through meaningful interactions, and how this interaction is transferred from one ghost hunting group to another <u>without</u> serious questioning its legitimacy.

This "process of engagement" (McLuhan 1964:22) at haunted sites becomes a uniform, mechanical, and repetitive one. For the most part, all the ghost hunter has to do is to be a passive observer to their tech devices, a non-participatory approach. Instead of innovative fieldwork at haunted sites, most 'ghost hunts' are 'dead ends'. There is little immersion into the complex 'hauntscape' process, occurring between sequences of situations, events, and experiences both in the past and present: what <u>happened</u> on site (as these site formation processes, both physical and socio-cultural) and the manifestations in the present (what is <u>happening</u> during fieldwork). Ghost hunting, as it is popularly practiced, has been a 'ghostgasm' because the 'hunt' in the field has been full of hubris, not critical thinking.

We don't need a hodgepodge of assorted ideas, beliefs, typologies, practices, and technologies that is a growing ghost hunting phenomena. We need a philosophy of concepts, and a work ethic, that valorizes the presence of a human past, one that ruptures the 'habit memory' of the 'edutainment' mold that is ghost hunting. Let's end the nostalgia of a 'ghost hunt', the illusion of cause and effect technological stimulation (and saturation), and the gross simplification of paranormal typologies of types of hauntings and ghosts.

In Japanese culture, for example, there are vast numbers and wide variability of spirits (cf. Figal 1999). In England, "there are more than two hundred ways of describing the ghosts" (Ackroyd 2011:7). Ghosts are not universalized entities who function in the same way and manifest for the same (usually negative) reason(s). Let's not reduce the semantically termed 'ghost' for different potential forms of ghosts. Let's end the continued adherence to dominant Western discourse for the definition, typology, and validity of these ghosts, which is largely controlled by various forms of ghost hunting social media representations.

We must not become attached to this framework of general typologies of ghosts and hauntings, such as genres of ghostly experiences, forms of haunting, and types of ghosts (cf. Waskul 2018). These are representations, lacking particular socio-cultural contexts and associations to other phenomena, as part of a relational haunting assemblage that may be embedded in a specific time, space, and place. Let's investigate these assemblages rather than illuminate commonalities and differences in these frameworks of typologies.

And let's not equate the use of technology at haunted locations with a more scientific approach. Bruno Latour (1993) has argued that much of scientific practice is based on a rhetoric of newness, yet is based on the idea that "annuls the entire past in its wake" (1993:57). Such tech use ignores the socio-cultural context of past site occupations, and site formation processes, replacing it with ever increasing new and improved technological saturation.

What these ghost tech devices offer, I propose, is what Bennett (2001) calls a "state of wonder" (2001: 5). Jeff Malpas (2012) has argued that this 'wonder' can evoke two modes of strangeness: in what form something appears, and as the manifestation in and of itself (cf. 2012: 260ff). These different modes of strangeness are significant at sites which 'entertain' both ghost hunters and archaeologists: the abandoned and the ruin, sites 'beyond' controlled emotion and order.

Both the ghost hunter and archaeologist sense 'wonder' at these places, but one is an invoked 'potentiality', albeit a 'ghostly' one by ghost hunters, as both modes of strangeness; and the other a strange, 'messy' stratigraphy by the archaeologist. In a ghost hunt, the strangeness becomes a presence of "sensorial agitation fostered through deliberate strategies" (Bennett 2010: 4, 10) as a technological means that provides meaning. This 'sensorial agitation' creates, I further propose, a "post-human media ecology in which a medium [ghost tech device] is understood as any entity that contributes to the becoming of another entity [a 'ghost in the machine'], affording and constraining possibilities of movement and interaction with other entities in the world" (Bryant 2014: 9). Bryant (2014) argues that "a number of different worlds exist and that [these] worlds are [the] ecologies of machines" (Ibid: 9). They are not, in most cases, ghostly human presences.

In ghost hunting, the 'wonder' becomes an still 'unconstituted past', a potential haunting, a 'normal' ghost hunting reaction especially in abandoned locations. In archaeology, at these locations of ruin and abandonment, there is a reorientation, from depth to surface as an archaeology *in* and *of* the present, creating an "unconstituted present" (cf. Lucas 2004), amid the wonder of a messy, disorientation surface debris.

This requires a shift in archaeology "away from the study of the ruin…and the abandoned to become a discipline which is concerned with both the 'living' and the 'dead'" (Harrison 2011: 160). But the 'normal' archaeological approach is still centered on what remains of the past in the present as material culture, not the dead as 'ghostly presences'.

In ghost hunting, the 'normality' in fieldwork centers on the use of ghost tech devices for investigating a 'haunted' site. All machines, including these ghost hunting devices, however, incorporate "operational closure", meaning "that a machine never relates to a flow *as it is* , but always transforms that flow according to its own operations and 'processes', those flows in terms of the internal structure of the machine" (Bryant 2014: 56). Thus, there is no distinction made by the machine between a natural flow and a 'paranormal' one. The 'wonder', in ghost hunting, is to make these ghost hunting tech devices (and apps) normal operating procedure.

Any association to fields of energy, its embeddedness in haunted space and/or attachment to a ghostly manifestation, is questionable. Bruno Latour (1993), among others, has demonstrated that energy, as something complex and systematic, exhibits many different forms of materiality (social, mechanical, environmental, to name a few). Any analysis of this energetic output requires ways that can define and separate these diverse processes (and their effects) from the complex network of entanglements of practices, technologies, and environments in which they are situated.

This challenges the paranormal view, espoused by ghost hunters, regarding the agency of anomalies as something paranormal, instead arguing that uncanny materializations and sensorial presences (including the investigator's themselves) co-create reality, including, I propose, that of a haunted space, and their construction of paranormal knowledge. We must be careful to too readily presume a 'paranormal' origin without embracing the human consequences of both ghost hunting methods and the haunted nature of sites that this creates in the form of potential future materializations at these sites.

The fallacy of the equation: tech device=scientific=verification of a haunting is also stressed by Nils Bubandt (2019) who states that ghost hunting taps "into the mystique of modern technology as a way of providing a solution to the magic of spirits" (2019:112). This is part of the "logic of the specter…that is at the heart of modern tech-gnosis, the mystical influence that technology exerts on modern society and the modern mind" (Ibid: 118):

"our environment, and I mean our man-made world of machines…is…beginning more and more to possess what the…primitives see in his environment: animation" (Sutin 1995: 183).

When individuals, such as ghost hunters, start to depend upon things and appropriate them as a central part of their fieldwork, a complex process is triggered. It results, again and again, in new creations, the 'ghost in the machine', as well as physical transformations in the way human practices are engaged (Hahn 2008) with these tech devices in the environment of a 'perceived' haunted location.

It creates a process of entanglement between the ghost hunter and these ghost tech devices. The device(s) become an integral part of investigative practices at these haunted locations, creating a "state of *relational entanglement*" (Stockhammer 2020:37), which "can also trigger an act of creation" (Ibid: 37), this 'ghost in the machine'.

This dependence upon these ghost tech devices has a 'rippling' effect in ghost hunting:

"It is the moment of encounter with a new or foreign thing [an 'uncanny' materialization] that forces us to give it a name [a 'ghost'], and this name influences our subsequent perception" (Stockhammer 2020:40).

Thus, on future 'ghost hunts, the same type of encounter ('uncanny'), using the same ghost tech devices, and their 'activation', creates 'haunting' manifestations at these so-perceived 'haunted' locations. The effect is a change in field practices and emotions. Ghost hunters becomes 'attached' to their ghost tech devices. This creates a basic entanglement of practice and perception: 'ghost hunting' = perception of 'ghosts' through the 'ghost tech devices'. These devices become 'technological witnesses', which serve as a basis for the creating of meanings (a 'haunted' location) and histories, albeit 'para-histories'.

Ghost tech devices are a return to magic, not a turn to

science: "the myth that they can act as portals [or at least permit it] to another world, another dimension of space itself" (Davis 2015: 197). These devices constitute an "effectancy", "they structure human action in a physical and psychical dimension" (Stockhammer 2020:43). The contemporary 'ghost hunt', even with its arsenal of electronic equipment and 'detecting' devices 'has never been modern'!

Ghost hunting certainly falls into the equation that "all societies [even groups] live by fictions taken as real" (Taussig 1987: 121).

Let's end the ghost hunting entrapment by its ideological focus on the 'object' (not 'subject' of inquiry): technology. It is so difficult for the contemporary ghost hunter, accustomed to their preset ways of conducting a 'hunt', with its polyrhythmic qualities of environmental deviations fostered by their technologies, to conceive of haunted space as anything but contemporary too. There is no conception of haunted space as a series or layers of surfacing presence within fields of social/cultural memory. Instead, haunted space is viewed and scanned/monitored as horizontal space, rather than being a 'deep map' of presences lying buried and surfacing.

This focus on the horizontal, clearly demonstrated by ghost hunts in abandoned, derelict, and now non-functional structures, creates what Edward Soja (1996) calls "third space", places recreated through imagination, materiality in ruin, and absent people. What is 'missing' (people and activity) is 'filled-in' through these horizontal tech scans that suggest (to ghost hunters) a change from absence to presence.

They create paranormal possibilities, as prefigured 'negative spaces'. This allows any 'sign' of presence (such as a tech device 'activation' or an environmental deviation) to be considered a haunting manifestation, without thoroughly analyzing all possibilities of agency. The resultant ghost stories, and their analysis, become 'para-histories'.

Thus, ghost hunting, using an array of scientific (and other) technologies, becomes an alternative to human history because it does not focus (for the most part) on the historicity of past site occupations, but rather contemporary 'para-history'. The past is not absent and gone. It is still present in what remains, and perhaps 'who' remains as someone still attached to a particular experience, situation, event, or habit within embedded fields of memory. And the future has always been a past present still.

By focusing on technological scans and monitoring/observation, ghost hunting does not involve this cultural context, nor an immersion (as participant) in past social contexts that occurred at the site. Participant-observation is a hallmark of ethnographic fieldwork, which ghost hunting certainly is not.

Then, there is the question of temporality. In a 'ghost hunt', time is always the present, and that temporality manifests in the form of contemporary behaviors, speech, and technologies, all brought to the 'host' site (the place under investigation). In this sense, the 'ghost' is the contemporary ghost hunting team, bringing an alternative way of 'being' and occupying the site.

Yet, there are alternative, and multiple, temporalities, even in now ruined and abandoned sites (cf. Dawdy 2010). These lie not only on the surface, in the form of material remains, but also those 'percolating' to the surface (as potentially both human ghostly presence and geo-environmental 'ghosts' of processes of distant antiquity). This opens the possibility of a 'haunting' to multiple agencies and processes.

As Dawdy (2010) suggests:

"Studying why and how ruins are not only made but also erased, commemorated, lived in, commodified, and recycled can tell us … much about the processes that created the original edifices".

The sites of ruin, much explored in 'ghost hunts' involves multiple processes and agencies, both physical and cultural occurring there, some of which happen simultaneously. These abandoned sites are still becoming 'present' with regard to presence. This expands the 'normal' limits of fieldwork at these locations. It demands a 'reset' of 'ghost hunting/paranormal investigation'.

THE 'END' OF GHOST HUNTING (AS WE KNOW IT)

Today's 'ghost hunt', no matter what form it takes (as tourism, 'edutainment', scientism, experimentation, or subcultural 'elitism') is not 'pioneering science', nor a baseline of scientific legitimacy. There is still no hard data, in the form of audio, video, or environmental readings, that validates the presence of a dead, human cultural ghost. Let's end the 'hunt' by beginning anew.

Let's begin by ending some major misconceptions and mis-directions. The dead are not in need of 'discovery', as a ghost hunter's 'Holy Grail'. A 'ghost hunting' goal is not to undue ghostly attachments in order to execute a 'releasing', a 'passing' to the 'other side'. Ghost hunters are not 'traffic cops', telling the ghost it is time to 'crossover'. This is undoing "complex social ties which once held the living person together" (Course 2007: 77), and some dead bound to certain spaces of this world. A new 'pastness' and 'deadness' should be enacted that 'goes beyond' the ghost hunting 'paranormality' and 'folklorization' of haunting phenomena.

The question is what new ways of knowing can we forge through an analysis of 'death'? How can we extract meaning from an exploration of what occurred <u>before</u> death (as individual biography), and what happens after death (the "necrography" (Panagiotopoulos et al. 2017))? How can we create a relationship between the living and the dead, their past biographies and their present state, as a necrography? This necessitates a novel approach that 'meshes' the two opposing states of being (biography and necrography), regarding haunting phenomena and identity.

The transition from death to 'other' has never been the focus of ghost hunting. There is an understanding of death as the end of the biological body. But this only hints at a partial understanding of what happens after death, where biology takes analytical precedence. The manifestation of intentionality on the part of the dead (as 'ghost') has largely been treated as something else.

While death is a social phenomenon, as socially-constructive closures through ritualistic acts (such as funerals), the dead are ignored as largely outside the social domain during most 'ghost hunts'. Ghost hunters treat the dead as 'things' responding to 'cues' and 'triggers' from ghost hunting questions and commands, technological activations from their ghost tech devices, and/or 'appearances' in space verified by environmental deviations. Where is the dead cultural being in these manifestations?

In "Ghosts of the Goldfields" David and Sharn Waldron (2019) say that "ghosts, in whatever manifestation they are encountered, are a window into the internal workings of the society and the individual" (2019: 230). Further, as Philip Clarke comments, "Spirit and ghost beliefs contain encoded knowledge about culture and landscape" (2007: 141). Both are cultural perspectives, which deviate from most ghost hunting 'ghosts in the machine' perspectives.

The 'hunt' is over. Let's end the masquerade: 'ghost tech' as investigator! Let's also go beyond subjective 'para-histories'. These para-histories are not history because they are fiction, without considerations of material culture or containing written historical narratives. They are woven through dark gaps and normal silences, filled-in by ghost tech devices. What these devices imply are not the voices and written words of people who have lived through past times. They are iterations of 'paranormal politics', displays on social media by observers (not investigators) of these tech device activations and measurements. This uncontrolled, and mostly useless data, ends history.

What this para history is actually describing is a form of temporality (or time) that is cut into tiny bits of data 'signals' that become recorded throughout a site, forming actualities of time in different configurations (environmental readings, EVP recordings, videos of darkened spaces, etc.), none of which are integrated in a meaningful relational configuration. They become a compilation of an archive rather than an investigative analysis, and is nothing more than experiencing the present tense of a site, not the presence of the past, the supposed (para)-history.

The only consideration worth continuing in the concept of 'para' is to 'go beyond' the 'ghost hunt', beyond the ghost tech devices, beyond the restricted territoriality of haunted sites controlled by particular ghost hunting groups, the 'expert' status of 'para-celebrities', the proliferation of paranormal TV programming, and the elitism of para-conferences. Their elimination can only help to make sense of the many layers and different agencies and processes involved in the production of a haunted site.

We must remember that ghosts are not 'things' (visual or auditory anomalies) and a haunting is not environmental deviations, shadows, acousmatic (unknown) sounds. They are not uncanny phenomena, or a product of the imagination. As Hans Holzer, "one of America's most high-profile ghost hunters" (Haining 2008: 480) once said: "Ghosts are people, or parts of people, anyway, and thus governed by emotional stimuli. They do not perform like trained circus animals, just to please a group of skeptics or sensation seekers", as in public ghost hunts.

Is 'ghost hunting' an accelerated form of fieldwork, exploratory acts in perceived haunted spaces, with largely a 'tracking record' of 'para-histories'? Is 'edutainment' really knowledge production? Is the use of ghost tech devices at these locations really 'advancing' the field, or is it instead a "competitive data-centric, technocratic [approach that is] alienated from the societies it serves and studies" (Cunningham and MacEachern 2016: 4)? Does the paranormal tech arsenal, as a 'fast science' tool kit with tech data logs of measurements and readings, create what Caraher (2015) calls a virtually meaningless mass of encoded data" (Caraher 2015: 433)? 'One night stands' at haunted locations, typical of most 'ghost hunts', is not the solution to a two millennium old (or older) question: Is this space/place haunted by ghosts?

Let's become more disciplined, 'slow down' the process of fieldwork. 'Slowing down' fieldwork counters the pursuit of assumed efficiency and suggests methods and practices that would stress interpretive (not technological) insight. 'Slowing down' calls upon ghost hunters to recognize the influence of speed through technology on ghost hunting. Harvey (1990) and Rosa (2013) have both observed that the accelerating pace of places saturated with technology have created new categories of experience and social relationships. Too often, as if it were a 'badge of honor and courage', ghost hunters talk and write about how many 'investigations' they have conducted at haunted locations: some confessing into the thousands, others three or more in a single weekend! This is as much a critique of their behavioral practices, as it is of their extensive use of ghost tech devices, and the way these 'tools' are used, described, and given power on social media.

One should be highly skeptical of the results of these scans and measurements, and the benefits these devices offer to greater efficiency, consistency, accuracy, and the production of knowledge at these rapidly-scanned haunted locations. The complexity of these sites, as layers of embedded and attached material culture, memory fields, and presence is enormous.

Missing in all of this 'hunting' and scanning' activity (much wasted time waiting for something to happen) is the 'craft' involved, a creativity in fieldwork practices. This craft is the uncovering of a particular cultural (both material and sensorial) presence that is no longer visible. This work involves not what you see, but rather what you cannot (yet) see. It is an archaeological sensitivity as that "capacity to anticipate what is not yet visible…the ability of *feeling forward*" (Simonetti 2014:4). Can this sensitivity also be used in the field at haunted locations, not as a 'psychic' ability but as the craft of this archaeological 'sense-ability' through the 'crafting' of sensible (and sensitive) context-specific performance practices?

We need alternative stories, that there are other ways to be told that a site is haunted, not merely through a 'ghost hunt', a tech version that produces the 'ghost in the machine'. Technology, as Neil Gaiman says, "does nothing to dispel the shadows at the edge of things". Ghost stories, as a site's 'para-history' "still hovers at the limits of vision".

We must also reconfigure our notion of 'materialism', be it uncanny, acousmatic, or haunting, to "a process in which objects and people are made and unmade, in which they have no stable essences [that can be measured with a ghost tech device, for instance] but are contextually and historically contingent" (Lucas 2012: 166). Ethno-historical context is important. That means, there is little or no accountability assigned to a 'para-history'. What we need is a relational process, and that relation is not what is done on paranormal TV programming. It is about an assemblage'.

The elements that make up this assemblage are important:

"the elements…also include the *qualities* present…and

the affects and affectivity of the assemblage: that is, not just what it *is*, but what it can *do*" (Wise 2011: 92).

The concept of "qualia" (cf. Chumley and Harkness 2013) is useful for fieldwork at haunted locations, especially in analyzing problems of the senses, embodiment, and affect. Qualia are "experiences of sensuous qualities [such as sound and smell, among others]…and feelings" [such as 'otherness'] (2013: 3). Qualia "are not just subjective mental experiences but rather sociocultural events of 'qualic' – and qualitative – orientation and evaluation" (Ibid: 3).

It is what counts contextually (as part of a site's ethno-historical-archaeological record), to the experiences of qualities of particular sociocultural layers of memories whose value is 'embedded' in material objects (cf. Munn 1986). Could it also be attached to particular spaces as sensorial residue? Do some sites have a 'haunting qualia', not related to a tech measurement or a ghost tech 'activation'?

Could this 'haunting qualia' create an "indexical icon" (Silverstein 1993: 52), a qualitative bodily state that is both the outcome of certain context-specific acts that create a sense of shared experience between a specific layer of memory and a space/site-specific act during fieldwork? Does this afford a different way of perceiving a haunting materialization, as a relational entanglement between a layer of past memory, space, performance practice (with/without a context-specific object), and contemporary investigator?

Does it alter the 'qualia' of meaning of the haunted site itself? It this because "instead of providing a simple means of delimiting the sensations [through ghost tech measurement of ambient change],…we consider…the experience itself [in that] which evinces it, the quality is as rich and mysterious as…the whole spectacle, perceived" (Merleau-Ponty 1962: 5)? Is this the effect of the relational entanglement, rather than simply an 'activation' coming from 'unproven' ghost tech devices?

The question we should be asking at a haunted site are what can manifestations do that actively produce contextual meaning (to what occurred at the site in the past) and affective associations. This, then, becomes a 'haunting' relational field.

This is a web of associations brought about by movements (cf. Ingold 2000) that can include physical actions, perceptions and sensory experiences, that focus on specific people, spaces, things, and other seen and unseen phenomena with respect to each other (Pauketat 2013).

These web of associations or entanglements are not merely engagements between various elements but their interpenetration that can transform particular experiences and places, such as the haunted site. This has the result that "any one movement is potentially an engagement with multiple points of articulation in multiple dimensions. Unraveling one entanglement means unraveling an entire tapestry…with meandering and citational strands of life and death" (Baires et al. 2013: 213).

This results in the development of place (such as the 'haunted' site) "in which not only events occur, but in which memories are also formed or reawakened, and experiences unfold…are increasingly recognized for their multisensory qualities…evoking a field of emotional response" (Brittain 2013: 259) that can 'haunt' the place.

These assemblages are "collectives or systems of usually familiar entities" (Lucas 2013: 375), such as those encountered by archaeologists during the excavation process. However, "when such assemblages start to act like independent entities themselves…at this point that we can cease talking in terms of networks or connections and must start talking of a new and emergent entity" (Ibid: 375) which I propose is a 'haunting' by 'ghostly' presences.

Then, there are the places frequented by contemporary ghost hunters. Much of this ghost hunting still copies from other ghost hunts and what is seen on TV, thus situating the field exercise as something both boring and entertaining, depending what is subjectively (or technologically) experienced. When we reduce investigative flow to a fragmented mix of serious, scary, passive, conversational, and entertaining elements, the end result is temporal, physical, and social displacement of encounters with potential haunted space.

And those who record and measure in the field, but analyze that data elsewhere, move the space of encounter (and the production of knowledge) elsewhere, where the disparate parts of the investigation become re-assembled into a new assemblage called a 'haunting'. This is the documentation of two spaces (the site of investigation and the site of analysis), not a 'paranormal' event. Thus, there remains a tension between habit, field practices, spatial disparity, and this lack of creativity: everyone is basically doing the same thing (and those who don't get criticized!).

Not all 'haunted' sites are hauntingly the same, nor should they be investigated in a similar manner. What is needed is a systematic organization of fieldwork that occludes a wide range of immersive practices (not surface scans) that preserve the context and the impact of practices beneath (and surfacing). Fieldwork at haunted sites must be grounded in the work of craft, not the efficiency and speed of tech scans. Slowing-down fieldwork allows us to really ascertain what these scans are measuring and recording. A 'slow down' approach requires an awareness, a bodied attentiveness (not a scan or measurement) of being in the place. It requires investigative practice as forensic analysis, a concern for details, where everything becomes relevant. This takes time and patience, not a rush to judgement, or to up the number of locations 'investigated'. It is working through layer upon layer that define a complex time and space haunting assemblage. This type of 'slow-moving' analysis can transform what today is merely 'ghost hunting'.

Also, these 'slow' immersions into potential 'haunted' space must be situated in an ethics of care, not amusement or entertainment, and co-becoming as working with what (and possibly 'who') remains of the past in the present. This ethical approach is critical to post-human (not 'para' or 'beyond') histories.

Bruno Latour (1993) has demonstrated that any effort to analyze the complexity of energy in any system, especially, I propose, in haunted space — be it social, mechanical, residual, or environmental – requires acts that define and separate energy and effects from their complex network of entangled relationships and practices: contemporary (as in ghost hunting tech scans), past (effects of these electronic scans from previous 'hunts'), sporatic, ephemeral, processual (geo-environmental), and media residues (cf. Parikka 2015), to name a few. All of these may be occurring at any one time, besides the possibility of a ghostly materialization:

"the residues of the accumulated energies expended…the signs of toil and the remnant artifacts of production…gives rise to a sense that all the invisible energy is stored somewhere…is trapped in the cold concrete floors or behind the walls" (Edensor 2005: 154).

Is this human 'ghostly residue', an actual 'ghost' manifesting, what remains of the 'host' environment, or the detection of what is merely brought to the site by past 'ghosts in the machine in ghost hunting?

Ghost hunting, I propose, as an aberrant form of transhumanism, considers seriously the interplay between technology and performance in society (e.g. Haraway 1984), as a vague roadmap of haunted space. The use of ghost tech in fieldwork creates a hybrid space, populated by 'ghosts in the machine'. The documentation of a haunted suite requires more than just simple relationships between 'ritualistic' technological scans and a way (through electronic activation) of producing (and recording) presence. Reproducing the same habitual interplay between investigator and tech device is the leading cause of 'paranormal paralysis' that has produced meaningless order in haunted space.

This 'machine performance', more often than not, eschews expertise and specialized knowledge necessary to analyze the possibility of a haunted space/site. The messy, mostly improvised 'ghost hunt', an interaction between tech tools, their effect, and the ghost hunter, becomes 'lost in translation' during the electronic performance in darkened, out of the way, places.

In this mess of presence, absent spaces become enclosures of paranormal presence, a designation that does not separate surface from depth, normal from paranormal, natural from supernatural, nor a 'hunt' from organized fieldwork. The concept of surfacing, vertical agency mixed with horizontal scans and measurements, misinterpretations caused by the ghost tech device, or its material components, the uselessness of monitoring 'surface' space without taking into account this depth, limits the development of a thorough investigative immersion into these haunted spaces.

We need to change the traditional (and 'normal') trope of exploring haunted sites as surface probes, as exercises in asking questions to an empty space, as scanning darkened spaces, and as monitoring a surface now abandoned. These exercises in 'edutainment' do not take into account what may be surfacing naturally, or even what may be emanating naturally from the materiality contained in the components of those ghost tech devices.

In ghost hunting, most of the presumed manifestations

of ghosts are 'purposeless ghosts'. They are 'summoned' by ghost hunters, or so they assume through their questions or their technologies. There is little hint at cultural context as intent when this 'summoning' occurs. Thus, these 'summoned ghosts' are also 'social-less' and 'culture-less', with no attachments ascribed by the ghost hunter to a particular space, situation, event, or layer of occupation at a site. This is because the 'summoning' is (most of the time) through non-context-specific questions and solicitations to 'affect' their devices, which is not socio-cultural in nature or contextual because it is not part of past experience and memory.

Ghost hunting sounds (and feels) different in its approach to the presence of the past, but what does it really accomplish besides entertainment and an ephemerality of emotions, at best? The 'hunt', as gathering, is more a social event, allowing boisterous 'high spirits', not ghosts, free reign. It is a convivial 'get together', masked as an 'investigation'.

Ghost hunting needs a new strategy, fit for serious research, a structured working environment. Let's be different, not 'paranormal'. Let's stop conducting the same old routine of asking irrelevant (and embarrassing) questions, monitoring empty spaces while waiting for something to manifest. Let's stop electronic scans. These scans only inscribe, through their internal materiality, a 'geology of media' (Parikka 2015) or 'media archaeological' (cf. Huhtamo and Parikka 2011) trace presence for future ghost hunters. These technological 'sweeps' and 'scans' extend a 'vibrancy' of presence to spaces beyond the 'hunting zone', affecting other sites of mediation through posts on social media:

"technologies have powerful but cultural specific effects, bringing into being new kinds of subjects, new modes of communication, new audiences and publics, and new notions of voice as personal and collective agency" (Weidman 2014: 42).

For example, what does the extensive use of a 'ghost box device' (or something similar) really detect: the voices of the dead or the transmission of these 'geologies of media' and 'media archaeologies' that are circulating through the atmosphere? Do they also create, through transduction, something perceived as beyond a human ghostly presence, perhaps, as perceived by some, the 'voices' of demonic presence? Let's stop registering 'anomalies' from acousmatic (unknown) agencies, simply to say that a ghostly presence has manifested. And let's not continue to 'window shop' for new devices to cover more 'technologically' the 'hunting ground'!

Isn't it more useful to begin with the known (as the cultural reality, not 'para-history', of a location's layers of occupation), and work backward (as archaeologists do). To do this, we need to separate ourselves from the typical mindset of a 'ghost hunt', and re-think our practices. Context is everything at a haunted site, as it is in archaeological excavation.

The very nature of a haunting implies a return of the past, the irruption of time into the present. The "ghost is often used to resurrect the past" (Smith 2010:76). This irruption is not a 'para-history' because "the ghost story…holds to a model of history as traumatically rather than nostalgically available to us" (Hay 2011: 15). This normally 'hidden history' uncannily returns in a haunting. It is not a history <u>beyond</u> us, a 'para-history.

Let's also end the concept that "a house with an unsavory history" (King 1982: 296) is a "bad place", or worse, a 'portal to hell', a theme so popular today on paranormal TV programming. A genuine haunted house "demands a [real] historical context" (Ibid: 309), not a 'para-history'.

Let's be 'punk' about all this and, at the same time, avoid the 'normal' paranormal footprint. Let's change the scene of fieldwork by becoming anti-establishment to the 'habitual acts' of 'pop' (popular) ghost hunting. We do this by being 'punk para-normal', that is, going beyond the 'normality' of a 'ghost hunt', the how to populate the haunted scene.

We begin by ending the 'hunt' for new technological mediums, as this has always been a problem. As John Durham Peters (1999) has said: "[e]very new medium is a machine for the production of ghosts" (1999: 139): each new medium has its own 'wardrobe malfunction'. Let's change the 'tune', tone, and ambiance of the 'normal' ghost hunt setting.

The link between modernity, science, and advancing technologies merely creates more 'ghosts' that "flourish in an eras you might expect them to be dead and buried, without a place. They are something brought about by modernity itself" (Dolar 1991: 7). That they do indeed flourish can be seen in the contemporary proliferation of different kinds of paranormal entities that are perceived out there in haunted space, largely through the tech devices used on a 'ghost hunt'.

Ghost hunters assume that ghosts are interpreting subjects acting upon passive non-human objects, their tech devices, a direct communication link, rather than recognizing that humans (including 'dead' ones) are just one of many entities that populate and interact in the world (Jones et al. 2013: 15). The ghost hunting devise, independent of 'ghostly' and human intervention, can, because of its material composition and handling, become "vibrant matter" (Bennett 2010) and activate on its own.

This ability to self-activate is part of 'new materialism' theory (cf. Bennett 2010; Harman 2005; Latour 2005, to name a few) that reality is intricately connected with other entities in nature and culture (other entities, phenomena, and processes, not exclusively to ghosts). New materialism calls into question all measurements and 'readings' that simply (and solely) link changes measured in the environment with the manifesting of human haunting phenomenon. Objects (such as ghost tech devices) in this new materialism 'turn' have an existence of their own, needing no activation by contemporary human or 'ghost'. This calls into question the validity of ghost tech devices (and other technologies) to solely detect 'ghosts'. Their usefulness in fieldwork becomes minimal, at best.

The use of ghost tech devices in fieldwork at perceived haunted locations is only part of a larger problem with ghost hunting. This is a difference between what there is (remains) at the site, which is ontology, and <u>proving</u> what is manifesting there (epistemology). According to Ribeiro (2019), "there should be a discipline that comments on what exists, and a discipline that comments on the knowledge of what exists" (2019: 27).

If ontology can be thought of as incomplete reality, and epistemology as a discipline that mediates what can and cannot be known, then ghost hunting combines, not separates, ontology and epistemology: ghost hunters comment, through social media and TV programming, what 'exists' at a haunted site (ontology), and the securing of that knowledge of what exists through ghost tech measurements, scans, and activations (epistemology). Ghost hunting chooses what is 'reality' at a haunted location (the 'para-history'), how to detect that reality (ghost tech), and the 'blanket' acceptance that what these devices gather is relevant data. Any deviations from this ghost hunting relationality of ontology and epistemology is meant with sharp criticism.

It is time to change (and separate) this vicious cycle of ghost hunting reality ('what remains') and how to document it (through what is being measured, scanned, monitored, and activated through these electronic devices). This would open the door to a different reality at all haunted locations. Haunted space is composed of various different 'actors' (the living, the dead, objects, technologies, the environment, to name a few), operating within various relationalities on an ontological level of reality.

Using this relational approach at a location (including a 'perceived' haunted one) means that "each phenomenon arises from the relationships comprising it" (Fowler 2013:2). This means "putting relationships first and thinking about how things, people, places, materials, ideas, properties, and so on *emerge from* those relationships" (Ibid: 2). It also "recognizes that the entities and forces involved in any specific event [including a 'haunting', I propose] have a history and that past relationships…have an effect in that event" (Fowler 2013: 2).

With several 'actors' and relationalities occurring in any space (simultaneously, erratically, ephemerally, sporadically), the ontology of potential 'haunted' space is a mess. A materialization may have a single agent or multiple agencies operating as an 'agentic assemblage'. All of these potential 'agents' of materialization are participating in the construction (as site formation processes) of the present reality at a haunted site. How can ghost hunters determine origin and type, especially when these materializations are largely trace, fragments, and ephemeral in nature? That is why simple typologies of 'ghosts' or types of hauntings, deemed universally applicable, becomes both ontologically and epistemologically irrelevant, since, using this "realist perspective", there is concern not only "with human experience, but with all of the relationships and media involved in any interaction" (Fowler 2013: 2), both past and present.

The "taxonomic fallacy" (Harman 2012) of these typologies is merely an assumption where "any ontological distinction must be embodied in specific kinds of entities" (2012: 189). Such taxonomic categories, based on subjectivities of association of unproven qualities of entities and places, creating a universal archive (the 'para-history'), helps little with understanding what may be occurring at a haunted location. Each haunted site has different "realist relational" (Fowler 2013) relationship assemblages because past histories, not contemporary 'para-histories, different from site to site (as location biographies).

A 'para-history' is merely the history of manifestations perceived, or conjectured from unproven ghost tech device 'activations', or from environmental scans that do not take into consideration other, 'normal' physical processes. This 'para-history' is not a location's archaeological record. This is what happens to ruins, abandoned buildings, and landscapes, once the locus of archaeologies in and of the present, now becoming increasingly the 'haunt' of ghost hunting and ghost tourism.

It demonstrates how contemporary archaeological spaces can become overlaid with folkloric and pop cultural interpretations that are at variance to a site's archaeological record and its occupational biography. This occurs through newly-inscribed histories of ghost hunters and ghost tourism which can create palimpsestual sweeps that, besides inscribing new experiences and memories, can erase or suppress (at paranormal 'hotspots') older inscriptions of historical presence.

In these 'para-histories', the presence of the past is largely subjective at best and useless at its worst. The 'effect' use of unproven ghost tech devices during a 'hunt' do not, for the most part, document a 'ghost' from the location's past, but may be recording (and measuring) the 'emotional' activities of prior 'live' ghost hunts. If so, this would reverse the process from cause = effect to effect = cause, a device causing a past 'manifestation' to the effects of these devices causing a future manifestation.

This becomes merely a transfer of presence from one ghost hunt to another. It is a different form of relational entanglement through lines of movement from one ghost hunt to another. It creates new 'haunting' assemblages at a location, 'bundles' of inscribed ghost hunting behaviors, dialogue, and technologies. The 'unnamed' ghosts, once difficult to ascertain because most have remained 'unidentified' by recorded history, now become the 'ghost hunters' of past 'ghost hunts'

There is no ghostly typology, for example, of forms of presence that incorporate the 'leaks' from the materiality of ghost hunting devices or the 'imprinting' of emotion by 'ghost hunting' onto the environment, as an emotional response to the 'activation' of their ghost hunting devices. These become remainders of contemporary presence that enter into a 'living' history (not as 'para-history') of a ghost hunt:

"might the touch of a body, the sweat of it, even the sound or gesture of it in some way remain as residue of/as the device itself, in the ongoing afterlife of contact"?

(Schneider 2019: 56).

"what residue of hand, sedimentation of use, drags along with this object?...of what other scenes, and other uses, now long obsolete…" (Ibid: 63) remain?

One example of this is the intrinsic link between shoes and their wearer. Are shoes imprinted onto the environment and imbued with the essence and personality of their wearer (Houlbrook 2013: 107-108), such that an ongoing series of ghost hunts at a particular site leaves 'signature footprints', as a form of paranormal presence (reflecting the personality of the wearers), that subsequent ghost hunters detect on their tech devices?

The problem is this: "How do we simultaneously identify with and differentiate ourselves from death and from others who adopt different stances and perspectives" (Panagiotopoulos and Espirito Santo 2019)? We must separate 'ghosts' from cultural death perspectives, what Panagiotopoulos and Espirito Santo (2019) call "necrographies". This means the relation "between the living [and their biographies] and the dead [their past biographies as 'ex-living'], and the dead's (the 'ghost's') present transforming state, their 'necrographies'" (Ibid: 2019). All of these examples of possible multiple actors can affect the perception of a haunted site.

It is more useful to approach a haunted location from the perspective of a site biography. Igor Kopytoff (1986) had suggested that buildings, things, and places can have their own biographies similar to people. This is particularly important when there is an emphasis on the social dimensions of these sites and buildings. Such an approach has an historical (not para-historical) perspective. This includes what remains today in the form of material culture and, I propose, other 'presences' (such as sensorial elements).

The 'remains' of 'ghostly traces', something 'paranormal' by ghost hunters, can become valuable today as a form of cultural heritage. This emphasizes the nature of variability and fluidity in a site (or building) biography. In this sense, a 'haunted', abandoned and no longer functioning site or building continues to 'live', even in ruin. They live socially not only by what still remains embedded/attached to the place, but also how people use them by granting them different meanings, not merely a site of haunting phenomenon. This, then, becomes a 'biography of life', not a site of death, as an 'afterlife' along paranormal/para-history dimensions. The question becomes: How do we approach the task of tracing lives and fates (as biography and necrography)?

Sandra Huber (2019) has said this:

"Different ghosts and spirits themselves…offer different methodologies depending on what a scholar is trying to accomplish" (2019: 17).

And, as Stanley Fish (1980), literary scholar, has written: "The field of inquiry is *constituted* by the questions we are able to ask" (1980:1). Ghost hunters 'normally' ask these same questions: "Is anyone here with us tonight?" "Can you show us a sign of your presence?" If ghost hunting begins with these simple questions, it will never come to "a relevant answer if…practices have not enabled us to produce a relevant question" (Stengers 2011: 373). Practices, both past and present (and their possible effects) come before these simplistic questions.

Are these the epistemological questions that should be asked in a serious investigation? I think not! That is why ghost hunting/paranormal investigation, especially how it is practiced in the field (as a form of 'edutainment') needs to be rethought and reconfigured.

It is not enough to depend on the unsettling nature of what happened at a site (such as a horrific event), and use it as a pretext on how to investigate a site, or use it to verify an experience or something that would 'trigger' a ghost tech device. It is more important to devise sound methodological (epistemological) approaches to address (not ask) questions about site formation processes, rather than exploring the accuracy or authenticity of a location's reported 'para-history'.

The investigator in the field must act convincingly in at least two simultaneous ways: in one space as past layered memory (as participant), and in what is presently manifesting _through_ those same practices (as observer). Both performances must be competently executed. This is a movement toward the examination of "broader issues of memory, identity, and autobiography in relation to a particular and local cultural experience" (Pearson 2006: 14). It is a move that places past presence at the center of inquiry, rather than 'reactions' and readings from ghost tech devices.

THE NEW 'NORMAL' PARANORMAL: 'PUNK PARA-NORMAL' ARCHAEOLOGY

What follows are a summary of practices that can be applied in fieldwork at haunted locations. It is about approaching similar questions that ghost hunting asks at these locations. But these are 'other' practices, coming from multiple distinct perspectives in order to create a new understanding of what may be occurring at haunted sites, a new 'para-normal'. It is also about pushing 'beyond' traditional definitions, typologies, and the 'normal' practices of doing ghost hunting, and doing archaeological excavation (the science that deals with the continuing presence of the past in the present).

If ghost hunting is not science, nor a baseline of scientific legitimacy, can other ways to determine the presence of the past in the present, such as archaeology, be applied to ghost research? Archaeologist Matthew Johnson (1999) has said that "if science is about the rational accumulation of knowledge, assessed in rigorous, systematic ways, then we [as archaeologists] are all scientists" (1999: 37). If a scientific approach discards earlier ideas (and theories) that are no longer workable, a pop cultural approach (such as ghost hunting), which regularly uses narratives to form 'para-histories', and continues to use unproven ghost tech devices to acquire data about a haunting, based on belief, emotions, and subjective experiences, is not a scientific approach.

Can a haunted site be framed, beyond the paranormal notion of a 'ghost hunt'? Can it be conceived within a concept of 'rescue operations', rather than 'edutainment'? What kind of knowledge does such a perspective bring concerning ethno-history, rather than a 'para-history? Does it bring any at all, or is it merely a variant, albeit a more detailed, immersive, and sympathetic form of 'ghost hunting'? Can we 'reclaim' ghost research from its pop culture perspective and make it relevant today (and in the future)?

Can a more archaeological sensibility to embedded/attached layers of memory, and an ethnographic sensitivity to multiple worlds, populated by both humans and non-humans, rescue 'haunting' research from the 'ghost hunt'? Can expanding the 'stage' play a crucial role? Is asking questions, other than the 'normal', "is anyone here with us tonight?" or "show us a sign of your presence!", important? Is "What do we preserve at these sites"?; "What do we convey and how?"; "What does sensory (as opposed to technological) experience tell us?"; and "What is the core of our research and fieldwork" relevant questions? We need fieldwork actions "in the realm of cultural meaning-making, performance, and communicative practice" (Deloria 2006: 16), processes that transform a haunted place from merely a scene of ghostly presence back to a particular layer of memory of a 'host' site.

The question of what a 'haunted' site is can be suggested by ghost hunters, but may be verifiable one day by those who will have done something else. A 'ghost', as that 'ghost in the machine', is not how, in the future, contemporary manifestations will be recorded, measured, and documented, but how fieldwork is able to deviate from the enforced boundaries set by restricted contemporary ghost hunting practices. In our fieldwork, our questions must center on a broader ecology of remains (beyond the material), and how they can become present.

This will become a punk para-normal approach that will negate the meaningless divisions inherent in binary categories (natural/supernatural; normal/paranormal; absence/presence; and past/present, to name a few). These are replaced by new conceptions "which privilege presence [in its multiple forms], the present [as the contemporary past], and the active agency of identified/identifiable ghosts [to include environmental processes, ghost hunting media residue, and ghost tech materiality] over absence, the past..." (Stevens & Tolbert 2018:48). This becomes a form of "punk archaeology" (Caraher 2014) that embraced the punk notions of performance as open to challenge long-held ideas and tropes of archaeological fieldwork. Ghost research also demands demands this "hybrid practice" (Meskell 2005) of 'punk' fieldwork.

An archaeological sensibility to the presence of the past

in the present is not enough. As Bettina Arnold (1999) has written: "The archaeological past is perceived as passive, fixed in time and place precisely because it is 'past'. The archaeological past is unable to speak for itself, to contest or transform interpretations of its configurations" (1999: 1). We need a framework to clarify the different ways of perceiving a site and being in a place, different from most archaeological practice, and different from 'ghost hunting'. There is no single reality, a single meaning to traces of the past in the present. There are multiple.

Let's begin to do fieldwork that is 'host' ('haunted site') responsive. Let's allow the site, not the ghost hunter, as a surrogate, to dictate the progression of its own investigation. Such creative punk approaches can counter uncreative ghost hunting in the pursuit of the presence of the past in the present. Participatory design methodologies (see below), such as a physical occupational enactment (rather than re-enactment) can heighten awareness, and should be encouraged, executed, and displayed in fieldwork (cf. Perry 2018: 222).

If one is going to complain about the way things are done, one must offer an alternative to replace it. This alternative must not follow the 'norms', even in the field of archaeology, the science of the past. The replacement for ghost hunting/paranormal investigation is what I call 'punk para-normal', inspired by both 'punk rock' and 'punk archaeology' (Caraher 2014).

A punk para-normal looks for better questions, not better answers: it performs, not monitors, scans, or measures. Performance practices involve actions, specific context-specific acts. You got to have the courage to go out there and DIY because no one, especially in the paranormal field, is going to give it to you. Let's reject conformity, marketed to us through paranormal TV programming and paranormal celebrities, as something new and exciting, improved, or innovative. It's not! Be punk. Be different.

A punk para-normal is situated within a broader "academic movement toward punk as an organizing structure" (Morgan 2015). One example of this is "edupunk" in which Morgan (2012) expands as an "interventionist ethic to disrupt and interfere with a consensus view of the past". A punk para-normal is using a punk ethos, its attitude, sensibility, and performance, to re-energize the experience of a haunting during fieldwork. It is thinking toward remainders, as alternative presences in a site's occupational record in order to reimagine field practices as forms of communication, rather than simply working with (and through) ghost tech devices and their activations, measurements, and readings.

This re-imagining of a communicative repertoire of practices is a promise to engage creatively (and artistically) with the traces of memory in all its forms, both residue and interactive, embedded and attached. It is the re-working of fieldwork, and its communicative outreach, to something other than the 'normal' practices of 'ghost hunting'. This 'punk sensibility' is founded upon the questioning and challenging of established "modes of thought" (Beer 2014: 29) that has come to be known as ghost hunting/paranormal investigation. This 'punk' approach "has a deep-seated discomfort with established ideas" (Ibid: 29). As punk para-normal investigators, let's be bold, open, inventive, communicative. Let's produce fearless data, stripping back from those interpretations at the edge of a ghost tech device.

This punk para-normal is an expressive politics, energizing in defying paranormal 'elitism', and the paranormal TV programming, and para-convention circuits of TV 'para-celebrities'. It is becoming AB-normal' to the everyday paranormal social environment and experience. This 'punk' persona marks us differently from the usual paranormal field of ghost hunting/paranormal investigation.

Punk para-normal follows certain performance scenographies of a punk aesthetic through haunting phenomena, as envisioned archaeologically. It involves a deep mapping of place through immersive cultural practices, many of which involve sound as 'cultural artifact'. It embraces places in ruin, and performance 'excavations' as destructive, hallmarks of both punk concerts and archaeological fieldwork. As in a punk concert, in punk para-normal the performance is meant to induce (produce) audience (the ghost's) participation.

Marginal spaces, central locations for punk rock performances, now become places to 'excavate' and map the various layers of a haunted site. Punks, in their efforts to defy and question the accepted practices of the music industry…punk rockers challenged expectations with their concerts. They engaged in theatrical…performances openly rejecting the …sets associated with pop music" (Caraher 2014: 131). In a similar way, a punk para-normal is meant to question and challenge the way 'ghost hunting, as a pop culture phenomena, investigates a haunted site.

A punk para-normal, unlike traditional ghost hunting, will not wait for something to happen, or sit around and casually view a monitor gazing at dark spaces. A punk para-normal investigation is about performances. Place, in punk rock, spoke of an intimacy with the audience, and in punk para-paranormal there is this same intimacy, without the intervention of ghost tech devices. Haunted sites, including places of ghost hunting and archaeological excavation, are, I propose, marked "by traces of their other purposes and haunted by the ghosts of those who have used them in the past" (Govan 2007: 139). Both ghost hunters and archaeologists are 'ghosts', as they both bring different behaviors in occupying, if only for short periods of time, these spaces. That is why a punk para-normal differs from the 'normal', almost habitual, ghost hunting, and the traditional trope of an archaeological excavation.

Let's use the 'emotional stimuli' suggested by Hans Holzer to become more 'intimate' with these haunted sites. This 'emotional stimuli' is, according to (Kundu 2011), receiving a "consensus among behavioural psychologists that certain, powerful human emotions are more likely to solicit responses from other humans (including those passed, if…they are still able to sense earthbound emotions)" (2011: 11). Kunda further states that "in order to move the field forward and explore more innovative methods, it might be suitable to apply this knowledge during paranormal investigations. Experiments…might be more successful if such emotions, or circumstances involving such emotions, are used…" (Ibid: 11). I agree, especially if it is combined with an archaeological sensibility to the various layers of memory at a site, and a sensitivity to context-specific scenarios that 'target' particular cultural-sensitive emotions embedded or attached to a specific layer of memory.

'GHOST HUNTING' IS <u>NOT</u> ARCHAEOLOGY/ARCHAEOLOGY IS NOT "EVIL"

What makes a place an archaeological site? When does a site contain an archaeological record in its biographical profile. Some archaeologists today investigate recent abandoned sites, as an archaeology in and of the present, beyond the trope of antiquity. Most archaeological sites may not be (ever be) truly sites of abandonment, and "all archaeologically recovered remains have been conditioned by abandonment processes" (Tomka and Stevenson 1993: 191).

Abandoned sites, and places in ruin, have also become the frequent 'haunts' of ghost hunting too. Let my emphasize, however, that 'ghost hunting' or 'paranormal investigation' (as a more 'specialized' form of 'hunt' with a wider range of tech equipment) is *not* a form of archaeology, even in these ruins and abandoned buildings, even as a sub-field of historical archaeology. This is so, even when some archaeologists advocate for a "historical archaeology that allows for the experiences of historic places to include their ghosts and hauntings" (cf. Beisaw

2016a).

April Beisaw, in a paper prepared for "Haunted Landscapes" session of the Society for Historical Archaeology in 2016, has titled her paper, "Historical Archaeology as Ghost Hunting". In the paper, she remarks that "to help archaeological narratives manifest the ghosts of place, we can learn from the ghost hunters who make a living by providing alternative histories of historic sites". I question her statement that ghost hunters 'make a living by ghost hunting'. Besides, these 'alternative histories' that ghost hunting provides are mainly 'para-histories', ones principally based on subjective experiences and unproven ghost tech device 'activations', and, for the most part, these histories are not contextual to a location's ethno-archaeological record. According to Coll Thrush (2011), a historian, hauntings are "clues to specific local histories" when they are "placed in conversation with fine-grained social and environment history" (2011: XXIII), which most ghost hunters do not normally research, or, if they do, it is done on a limited basis.

In a paper in the book, *Lost City, Found Pyramid* (2016:b), she states that "tales of ghost hunters are full of suspense and everything else that archaeology used to offer" (2016: 186). As an archaeologist, with fieldwork dating back to 1969 (Wolvesey Palace, Winchester, UK). I take offense to that statement. Ghost hunting is not full of suspense, just speculation. And for me, archaeological fieldwork still 'offers' what I experienced back in 1969.

In a time when 'we are all archaeologists now' (cf.

Holtorf 2016), is it really necessary to incorporate a 'ghost hunting' perspective into the field of archaeology? Such a comparison is especially problematic when archaeologist Michael Shanks (2007b) suggests that there is potential for revealing the many stories, albeit many uncanny ones, which can be told about archaeological data. This is part of "an increasing trend… which might be understood as evidence of an archaeological 'Creative Turn'" (Lee et al. 2017; Russell and Cochrane 2014), as a way of "feeding an archaeologist's vision to the public" (Harrison & Schofield 2010: 117), rather than the 'ghost in the machine' stories of many ghost hunts.

Those archaeologists exploring contemporary ruins and buildings, as an archaeology in and of the present, making their way through dimly-lighted spaces where presence is absent, certainly experience the uncanny nature of these places akin to the experiences of ghost hunters. These places constantly make us aware of things and spaces as 'other', material 'out of place', as in a haunting (cf. Petursdottir 2014). As anthropologist Michael Taussig (1993), as part of the human condition (not just ghost hunting and archaeology), has said pertinent to this exploratory experience of the contemporary ruin:

"a configuration of very object-prone exercises in differentiated space, in which the thought exists in imagined scenarios into which the thinking self is plummeted" (1993: 33).

Contrary to what Beisaw (2016a) has implied, contemporary archaeologists no longer neglect the public's perception of their work. This awareness has resulted in the development of new exciting fields never previously offered by archaeology. These include 'community archaeology' (cf. Marshall 2009) and 'archaeological ethnography' (cf. Hamilakis and Anagnostopoulos 2009), among others. There is also more affinity between site-specific performance practices, such as 'theatre/archaeology (cf. Pearson and Shanks 2001), than there is between archaeology as 'ghost hunting', a link Beisaw (2016a/b) makes.

She further states that "ghost hunters, and the ghost stories they tell, are just one model of successful interaction between experts and their audience". Who is the 'audience' in a 'ghost hunt': the 'ghosts' or other 'ghost hunters'? Let's define 'successful interaction' and what is its effect toward the acquisition of real historical knowledge production? Finally, are 'ghost hunters' considered 'experts'? What are they 'experts of/in?

She states that a "democratized ghost hunting…can be performed by anyone with little training and no special powers", such that "one can become a ghost hunting professional within a matter of weeks" (2016b: 186)! What is a 'ghost hunting professional'? How is anyone considered an 'expert' with 'little training', 'no special powers', and become a 'professional' in a 'matter of weeks'?

"A ghost hunt…upon arriving a professional gives visitors a quick overview of the site's history..The professional will explain how it [a manifestation] does or does not fit within the known history of the site" (Ibid:

186). Much of this site history, however, is in the form of subjective 'para-histories'. As archaeologists, we do not believe that history need become a spectacle, as it is in many ghost hunts, to better communicate with the public. Instead, archaeologists today use the theatre's potential to create more comprehensive experiences that connect the past and present more contextually.

Rocco Bosco (2016), in an article on Ghost Archaeology in Australia, talks about this historical perspective of ghost tours there. He states that, while some tours use historical information on their tours, many avoid presenting historical knowledge in favor of tales of the supernatural. This redefines the site from a historical location to a paranormal landscape.

Who is the 'professional' on these ghost tours, the 'ghost hunter'? The known history of the site is usually filtered through the known 'para-history', which basically is based on subjective experiences and unproven ghost tech device 'activations'. Beisaw further states:

"Ghost hunters reclaim historic sites, museums…for the non-elite members of society that they see as under-or un-represented in museums." Really? Yet, later in the text, she states that "the emotional experience of encountering the ghost was more important to them than creating a historical narrative of the forgotten". This contradicts her previous statement.

She also considers ghost hunters better storytellers than archaeologists:

"Archaeology as ghost hunting is just an approach to

telling good archaeological stories" (2016b:193). This is because, she proposes, "archaeological ghost stories do not need to be fleshed out with historical facts…for ghost hunting works best when the stories are simple and incomplete". Thus, "archaeologists can improve their storytelling skills by learning from the success of ghost hunters" (Ibid: 186). So, archaeologists can improve their storytelling by telling stories that are "simple and incomplete", and become 'successful' as in ghost hunting? Really?

Archaeological storytelling has changed in the last decade or two. These changes, however, do not relate to 'simple and incomplete' stories as in ghost hunting. These changes do provide new meanings to the study of the past by relating their importance for identity and memory:

"The identities and memories, spatialized within the context of the field site, will always remain an implicit part of archaeological field experience and therefore should necessarily…be made explicit in the construction of place narratives" (Brown 2016: 20).

This is because "archaeologists occupy a powerful and privileged position: they exercise enormous control over memory and identity through ways in which stories of the past are told" (Ibid: 50). Can a 'ghost hunter' similarly 'exercise enormous control over memory and identity' in their telling of ghost stories? We, in archaeology, do have good, successful archaeological storytellers, so we don't need a 'archaeological ghost storyteller', in the tradition of ghost hunters to expand archaeological interest and readership to a more diverse general public.

One example is Adrian Praetzellis's, *Dug to Death: A Tale of Archaeological Methodology and Mayhem* (2003). This book introduces the reader "to the hows and whys of archaeological field methods in an entertaining but informative way". Mary and Adrian Praetzellis have been noted for their "archaeologists as storytellers" sessions at professional archaeological meetings, dating back to 1997 with a Society for Historical Archaeology presentation.

Also, a recent book, *Subjects and Narratives in Archaeology* (2015), continues this storytelling tradition. In the book, "the authors seek to move beyond the customary limits of archaeological prose and representation". Public outreach, authenticity, and art are cited for this new storytelling tradition in the form of "fiction, creative nonfiction, drama, visual arts, and other forms of storytelling [that] can powerfully convey ideas to non-specialists who are interested in archaeology". Jonathan T. Thomas, in his article in the book, "The Archaeologist as Writer", argues that if archaeologists do not write engaging narratives for the public, others will and will do it poorly. Is he referring to ghost hunting 'para-historical' accounts? Archaeologists do not need 'archaeological stories' told in the form of 'archaeology as ghost hunting'. We, as archaeologists, make our own good 'archaeological stories'.

Finally, Beisaw (2016a) says the following:

"Archaeology as ghost hunting is a way…to create engaging site-specific history lessons…Archaeology as ghost hunting…makes them *visible* to our audience. It tells a compelling tale …without providing unnecessary details. It leaves open spaces…It is memorable.. Archaeology as ghost hunting is about doing what we do…"

Does ghost hunting really 'create engaging site-specific history lessons, or speculative, subjective para-histories? Is ghost hunting really about what archaeology does, how their data is gathered and archived, and how they transmit that data, mostly through 'memorable' but unsubstantiated, social media presentations. I don't think so. That is why ghost hunting is not archaeology, and archaeology is not ghost hunting!

Beisaw's (2016a/b) remarks that liken archaeology to ghost hunting, a conception of archaeology as deficient, too easily allows ghost hunting to serve purposes that she says appears to be lacking in archaeology. As Assaf Nativ (2017) has stated, this puts archaeology "into the grinder of reverse engineering that seeks to discover what it [archaeology] once was, but in the process neglects to consider what it is" (2017: 660). Nativ considers that much of this is do "to a confusion of absence with loss" (Ibid: 660).

Archaeology is a discipline in which data is lacking, fragmented, and deficient. It involves a cultural record without 'live' actors and performances. We don't need 'para-histories' to fill the void, especially when these histories themselves are lacking meaningful contexts: physical, social, and temporal.

In archaeology, authenticity is obtained through context, the traces and fragments that remain of the past's present.

The value of this material that remains, for archaeological knowledge to be authentic, depends upon its removal from present context. What is the context of a haunting manifestation in ghost hunting? It is its relation, for the most part, to contemporary technological scans and measurements, and ghost tech activations? Is that a removal from present context?

What ghost hunting does, in contrast to the context of archaeological knowledge, is to mix up the past with emotional spectacle and 'edutainment' interests of the present. The result is that any manifestation, perceived as past presence, is not the same type of context concern as is the production of the past in archaeology.

If ghost hunting is 'edutainment' (at best), what use is an entertaining experience to archaeology in the production of knowledge about the past? Archaeologists exercise choice in their selection and gathering of archaeological data (and archaeological experiences) for archaeological purposes. What is the archaeological purpose (if any) of a 'ghost hunt'?

The 'haunting' character of the past in archaeology is not the same as it is in ghost hunting. In archaeology, it centers around the changes we perceive in the presence of the past in the present. In ghost hunting, haunting phenomenon is the 'un-changing' nature of the manifestation from past to present. Past presence in a haunting manifestation is not, for the most part, a transformation through time to the present. This unchanging quality in haunting phenomenon translates to similar 'para-histories' from site to site in ghost hunting. Local context becomes irrelevant. That is why there are typologies of ghosts, haunting phenomena, and types of haunted sites, no matter the country or culture, in ghost hunting.

In archaeology, the present past is not much like the way it was (in the past). The appearance and content of past presence has changed, its context has been transformed by site formation processes through the years, decades, and centuries. That is why present context in archaeology becomes important, while past context should be important in ghost hunting. Haunting phenomena is most unlike the archaeological present past.

Further, if archaeologists wait passively for the past to appear, like ghost hunters do during 'vigils' and site monitoring, nothing of that presence of the past would appear during archaeological fieldwork. Archaeology does not need to be ghost hunting! As Moore (2013) has said:

"Archaeologists go into strange unusual places…and many of them are susceptible to their emotions, their imagination…Many will tell stories of places that spooked them so much they had to leave, others talk of nightmares while excavating graves. Many a lab technician has heard things go bump in the night and day, especially when human remains are on tables or in boxes nearby. Spookiness and archaeology go together" (2013: 210).

Cornelius Holtorf (2008) describes "archaeology as an adventure" while on a dig at Monte Polizzo in western Sicily:

"Some of the most fascinating and memorable

discoveries and explorations of the fieldwork season took place both in the local town of Salemi and in the basement of the dig house itself" (2008: 153).

He describes how "we were living on top of 'a classic horror film scenario'. Unsurprisingly, one or two students subsequently experienced nightly spooks" (Ibid: 154). He goes on to say that "archaeological fieldwork is not only the sum of applied methods and techniques but also an experience that is significant in many ways other than what it purports to be" (2008: 154). This is the socialization process of an archaeologist.

Archaeology does not need the storytelling 'skill' of a ghost hunter. We have our own from the day and night experiences and stories that are created in the field. We have our own alternative histories that we experience at times as uncanny encounters during fieldwork. And we certainly offer suspense and everything else that ghost hunting can offer, and something much more: CONTEXT and 'in situ' excavations of past presence! Ghost hunting is certainly NOT about what we do!

Gavin Lucas, archaeologist (2001) has said this:

"The moment we put a pick in the ground, we are potentially bringing something new into the world, something that has never been seen before…" (2001: 142).

That to me is something that has never been done during a 'ghost hunt', and it potentially happens every time than an archaeologist excavates new ground into the past! It is about imagination which "is at its most powerful…in writing that could be said to be archaeological, that digs down in the dirt to bring other worlds back to life" (Wallace 2004: 12). That is not ghost hunting, which, in its quest to recover the human remains of past presence (a 'ghost') is more like 'antiquarian' study than archaeology.

This 'antiquarian' study involves the collection, measuring, and recording of objects in isolation (visual and auditory anomalies; environmental deviations; ghost tech device 'activations'). In contrast, archaeology is the study of remains, the past in the present, in their context, a specialized sense of systematic exploration through survey and excavation. It is a question of meaningful knowledge production (archaeology) vs. 'exploitation' in ghost hunting, the usefulness, in many cases, of the 'hunt' to gain recognition and 'ego-tripping'.

Archaeology still offers what Wallace (2004) calls " archaeological poetics", a "reading between the lines, appreciating what is buried, comparing present significance with past and now lost significance" (2004: 50). This requires the "archaeologist to see things in a new way, to turn the imagination 'inside outwards' in order to ponder what is hidden below the earth rather than what is visible above" (Ibid: 50).

Today, however, archaeology can be beneficial to ghost research, but not as ghost hunting. At sites of ruin, in abandoned buildings and landscapes, as an archaeology in and of the present, the 'excavation' of these sites, as potential 'haunted' places, archaeologists can "attend to the past" (Shanks 1995), in ways to determine the still 'active' presence of the past.

'Haunting' phenomena, like other archaeological knowledge, has to be produced. As archaeologist Michael Shanks (1995) has said:

"Acting upon, attending to the past, producing knowledges of the past: these are dimensions of archaeological experience…there would be no 'real' past without them" (1995:14).

But this archaeological process and archaeological experience in the 'excavation' of haunting phenomena will differ from the present tropes of archaeological fieldwork, but not differ from its archaeological sensibility and sensitivity to context and performance. This difference will be discussed in the next section. It is also a difference between this 'ghost archaeology', and its perspective of context-specific performance 'excavations', and 'ghost hunting'.

Finally, there is the problem of 'evil archaeology'. In a recent book, *Evil Archaeology: Demons, Possessions, and Sinister Relics* (2019), author Heather Lynn, considers herself a "renegade archaeologist" by assuming a 'punk' position: 'exposing' "hidden history, challenging the accepted narrative found in mainstream history books". The title suggests, at least to me, that archaeology itself is evil, or that archaeologists excavate (for the most part) 'evil' artifacts.

Her 'evil archaeology' is not contemporary archaeology, or a sensitive/sensible approach to what archaeological fieldwork unearths. In the book, there are various mis-matched stories between archaeological fieldwork and artifacts. Archaeological context is not substantive, and there is little, or all-together missing, referencing of sources. Finally, there is no relational (or rational) associations that differentiate these 'representations' of objects and their ontological context within past societies.

As David Parkin, in *The Anthropology of Evil* (1986) says, There is one major objection "that some anthropologists [and archaeologists] might have to defining an area of interest through the use of a concept of doubtful analytical value" (1986: 2), such as this 'evil archaeology'. He states that it is "still analytically more fruitful to approach the problem from the viewpoint of a particular 'concrete' activity (Ibid: 2).

He further states that "what people regard as being good or bad…may depend less on the relation [for example, between an archaeological object and its representation] than on other fundamental ideas, each specific to the culture, such as those concerning the nature of death and its relationship to life" (1986: 2). This would include "first principles of cause, effect, process, and transformation" (Ibid: 2). We must first know the ontology of a culture and its cultural artifacts before we know what they meant by those representations of evil. It becomes a question of relational associations between objects and their more than physical representations.

That is why we need an 'other' archaeological connection at these 'haunted' locations, one that is not based on subjective similarities between archaeology and ghost hunting, and one that provides context to artifactual patterns and assemblages. It is a 'ghost excavation' that does not focus on, at these 'haunted' locations, for 'portals to Hell' or the manifestation (or representations) of demonic presences. If not, the result will be the same as in contemporary ghost hunting: the 'evil' in archaeology complements the presence of 'demons' in ghost hunting!

PUNK PARA-NORMAL: 'OTHER' ARCHAEOLOGICAL CONNECTIONS

Can a 'detachment' from a building or place, something that affords ruin and abandonment, still maintain 'attachments' that result in future materializing presence? Does an entanglement between human and place remain as 'afterlife event' in fields of presence? Does this 'afterlife' attachment leave (besides material presence) non-material signatures on these abandoned buildings and places, in the form of 'haunting' sensorial assemblages? Are these 'haunting' assemblages integral components of these location's site formation, be it an 'afterlife' process?

An abandoned building/site's biography provides a powerful tool for exploring these locations, especially those perceived as 'haunted'. It is to recognize these locations as still 'living' in once lived spaces. What is needed is a hybrid, disciplined approach, not your 'normal' ghost hunt nor the 'traditional' tropes of archaeological fieldwork, including those of an archaeology in and of the present (cf. Harrison and Schofield 2010).

Such an approach would consider the history of events and practices at these locations, but not their 'para-histories'. Also to be considered would be the social memories (including habitual and repetitive behaviors) created and linked to these events in spaces of each location (cf. Mills & Walker 2008), and the connections between assemblages in various taskscapes, and the sociality of these acts in performing these various tasks (cf. Ingold 2000).

This attempt to 'excavate' memory is an archaeology of knowledge (Foucault 1972) that connects with specific forms of memory work (cf. Mills and Walker 2008). Like Foucault's archaeology, it examines how certain social rules (such as the 'good death', cf. Sabol 2014) order thought and relate to contemporary materializations at haunted locations.

Documenting this phenomena, through space/site-specific performance practices recognizes them as a class of sensorial 'artifacts' (such as past 'soundmarks' of a battlefield soundscape; cf. Sabol 2013) created through human action in the past (such as death on a battlefield far away from home; buried in unknown graves; cf. Sabol 2017) This creates an 'other' archaeology that still matters, even though it currently lies outside the mainstream archaeological tropes and, for that matter, outside the 'normal' ghost hunt (and its reliance on ghost tech devices to document this phenomena). That is why I call this approach punk para-normal, something beyond traditional archaeological exploration and a ghost 'hunt'.

A similar approach is Gonzalez-Tennant (2016), who 'excavates' folklore (as 'ghost story') as it relates to the tragic history of Rosewood, Florida, and the various meanings attached to the site. He shows "how past hatred can imbue a place with an eerie presence, a historic residue lingering in forms of evidence rarely examined by archaeologists. Rosewood exists as a literal ghost story haunting Florida's collective memory" (2016: 218).

He is, however, "not interested in inanimate intentionality but rather the ability of landscapes to influence humans and to continue to haunt them" (Ibid: 219). In that respect, it differs from the punk para-normal space/site-specific performance practices, context-specific to particular layers of past memory that may be embedded/attached to a haunted location in the form of sensorial 'artifacts'.

The question is: What remains (if anything) sensorially from past performances in these taskscapes? Are these sensorial 'remainders' (if they exist) as unrecorded (or ignored) archaeological remains that can reveal new entanglements as assemblages of 'haunting phenomenon'? Are these entanglements, if they exist, a form of intangible cultural heritage?

This brings us to a new set of questions not asked in a 'ghost hunt':

- How was an abandoned building or site transformed during this process of 'detachment' and 'attachment'?

- How are structures of abandonment and abandoned sites used by these newly attached 'haunting assemblages'?

- How can we study these questions, and provide meaning to what people may be experiencing at these locations?
- How does this approach differ from ghost hunting and archaeology?

These are important questions for any fieldwork that is conducted in these abandoned buildings and at these abandoned sites of ruin.

Coll Thrush (2011) has also identified some basic questions regarding whether places have ghosts/spirits. These include:

- "Can a single place be home to a certain kind of history…even across boundaries of time and cultural regime?"
- "Can remnants of past societies —ruins, ecological footprints, artifacts — 'speak' in active ways for the histories they represent?"
- "Can we include the dead, or apparitions of the dead, in this agency?" (2011: 54).

Today, "the past is no longer what it used to be", not even the past at haunted locations, and "neither is the academic study of the past" (Lorenz 2010: 67). Today, time is no longer linear: it "doesn't flow; it percolates" (Michel Serres). There is no one single time, but multiple. This means that an event does not merely occur in the present, it also simultaneously actualizes remains of the past within it. This actualization occurs, I propose, through context-specific acts, not tech scans or measurements. In archaeology, there is a "consideration of the contemporary surface as an amalgam of all layers of history" (Harrison and Schofield 2010: 52), including the "recovery of memory [and] the uncovering of the concealed" (Ibid: 52).

Historical time, in a 'haunting, is not 'para-history. It is part of the entanglement of time (one of many temporal lines). History is thus the present, not something that came before (a past that is gone) or something beyond (as 'para-history'). It is the here and now of things, places, and entities, both human and non-human (but not never human, such as demons and other such entities). The past is still present through its vestiges. In archaeology, this means material culture, but…. Are some past traces the vestiges of specific presents and presences that are not part of this material cultural trope? Do these other 'vestiges' occur at locations perceived to be 'haunted'?

The basic question that I seek meaning to at haunted locations is part of a 'classic' archaeological field operation: how do some members of a society (ghost hunters) treat the dead that reflect their basic belief system through the use of material culture- ghost tech devices, and audio and recording tools as 'scientific' instruments – that they assume can 'detect' post-human (ghostly) presence? Are ghost hunters witnessing and experience a 'ghost' (a biologically-dead human), or a new kind of 'ghost' that is abstracted from an old kind of process- 'residue' (ghost tech "zombie media" (Parikka 2015); environmental processes), not real past 'signatures' of a human 'ghost', but rather those of previous 'ghost hunting' activities?

The residue of old and older ghost tech devices can create a new future layer of this "zombie" residual, 'returning' traces at paranormal 'hot spots'. This 'zombie' residue is, more and more, replacing the human ghost as an (un)-dead 'body' of electronic residue at media-driven haunted locations, and sites of intense ghost tourism. As Jennifer Gabry (2011) has said: these "electronic fossils…provide traces of the economic, cultural, and political contexts in which they circulate" (2011: 7). These contexts are paranormal, not ethnographic.

Are these ghost tech traces, as 'zombie media', fragments of presence as waste, the 'ghosts' of the future, replacing human history and memory? After all, they are carriers of memories of the past that can come back to haunt the future. By their material duration in a 'waste' state, they continue to 'live' after their 'life' of functional usage has ended. They become revenants. In the future, will their 'dump sites' become perceived as new haunted locations? They do carry potentialities of a haunting in that they contain, in the storage devices of their hard drives, the existence of a past world(s), including human cultures, biographies, and events.

These short-term technological ruptures, as a 'zombie' trace, make indelible new marks onto the topographies of traces of presence at haunted locations. They mix with the electronic and emotional traces of previous 'hunts', producing a confusing mess between ghost tech/investigative residue, environmental residue, and the possible presence of the past (as human ghost).

An example of this environmental residue is cited by British archaeologist Miranda A. Green who has pointed out a connection or olfactory synergy between rotting wood and flesh. In many traditions, this is regarded as "still retaining part of the original life-force' (2004: 90).

Is the increasingly use of technology by ghost hunters 'speeding-up' research, fieldwork, and interpretation, as a product of technological efficiency, a good thing, or merely a shift from a post-human that 'haunts' with a purpose, to a disruption of space through environmental deviations documented by technology? Has the contemporary perception of a ghost become bits of data, snapshots of video, audio, photographic data, that is experienced and re-posted in virtual space, rather than the physical space of a haunted location? If this shift in perception is true, it does make ghost hunting more akin to archaeology, which is "the discipline that excels in recombining small fragments into new patterns" (Dawdy 2019: 190). But, today,

The "fundamental premise of conventional archaeology which posits that the reality of the past can be reconstructed on the basis of material remains it has produced simply does not hold" (Blaising et al. 2017: 6). This is because "there is no essentialized, naturalized, neutralized 'archaeology as such', no single archaeological lineage…over the last century, its conception of that 'study', those 'records', and that 'past' (and whether it is exclusively 'human') has evolved considerably. Archaeologists have questioned their own agency, the agency of their human subjects, and the agency of nonhuman creatures and objects in the archaeological terrain…Does the archaeological record exist 'out there' to be excavated, or do archaeologists create those 'records' by deciding where to sink the shovel…?" (Mattern 2017).

Does this open the door, is this a opportunity for other, non-material, approaches to the presence of the past in the present? Lucas (2012) has said that this archaeological record is a form of memory (2012: 210). If archaeology is about, all about memory (cf. Olivier 2011), why have archaeologists shown little interest (and even less regard) for spaces and sites that have been constructed, passed through time and remembered, manifesting this memory today in ephemeral, sensorial ways? Shouldn't archaeologists try to "learn what things and places remember" (Fowler 2013: 51)? Fowler (2013) further comments: "things do not only remember past events and assemblages, they actually continue the active presence of some of their constituent relations and events" (Ibid: 51). If this is true, why have archaeologists, for the most part, not studied ruins and abandoned sites said to be haunted, and the assemblage of things contained there, as possible sensorial 'remainders' of the past?

Why have archaeologists not explored more fully the past emotional states of a site's archaeological record? Why has "the literature on the archaeology of emotion and affect…mostly quite recent and…not extensive' (Tarlow 2012: 169)? Some of this literature is outlined in the following paragraphs. Much of this research "has mostly involved studying the shared emotional codes and standards that define a time and place" (Ibid: 179). This is called "emotionology" (Stearns & Stearns 1985).

This is part of a recent 'emotional turn' across both scientific and humanities disciplines that gives more awareness to the effects of emotions in providing meaning to human experiences in the past, particularly in the field of archaeology (cf. Gosden 2004). There are various examples of this archaeology of emotion approach in the archaeological literature. These include Harris (2010) who argues that places can become 'sticky' with emotions. He uses the emotional and mnemonic geographies of Hambledon Hill, a Neolithic site in the UK as an example. Ritual deposits in the landscape there helped to create emotional experiences, over multiple generations, of certain events and relationships. Does these remain as residue that still percolate in the present as a form of 'haunting'?

Foxhall (2012) has said that "objects can be charged with emotion in their own right, as well as being manifestations of emotionally significant relationships". Can they lead to an 'attachment' to place by certain groups or individuals, creating a potential (future) haunting manifestation? Can we use the material culture, specific 'emotional' artifacts, left behind in a ruin or abandoned building, to afford a past presence becoming present? These emotional artifacts would have to be context-specific to a particular layer of experience and memory that occurred at the site in the past.

This is part of a wider, and deeper, view of possible reasons for an embedded ('residue') and/or attached (interactive) haunting. It is "exploring emotional significance as something inherent in the designed properties of a thing as well as exploring accretion of emotional meaning through object biographies and context" (Tarlow 2012: 180). This means that there is a continuity between people and things. Something of their being, intentions, and personality are spread out, both spatially and temporally through traces associated with this relation between people and things (Gell 1998).

A recent example of this is Herva (2014), working with the materiality of Second World War German material heritage in Finnish Lapland. According to Herva, "military equipment..would have "abducted" (Gell 1998) qualities of the German army as a collective entity, and are still more or less residually charged by those qualities" (2014:306). This means "that the German troops left behind pieces of their relationally constituted selves...[that] continues to live in Lapland in the form of German *materiel,* mingled with landscapes and resulting in the 'percolation' of time...or a living-or haunting-presence of the past in the present" (Ibid: 306). She states that "things become alive-or their agency is activated-when people come to interact, in whatever form, with wartime sites and things" (Herva 2014: 308).

These military sites, she suggests, are like industrial ruins (Edensor 2005), the 'haunts' of much 'ghost hunting', and are "kinds of special places that afford sensory and bodily experiences which are different from...the experiences afforded by carefully controlled and ordered...environments" (Ibid: 310), and sites of controlled archaeological excavations. Such sites challenge the 'normal' order of things The experiences at these sites "allow some degree of restructuring the relationships between self and world and the present and the past" (Herva 2014: 318). In a similar perspective, Cynthia Landrum (2011) establishes a link between haunted ground, material culture, and 'undead' histories. Such an approach complements the process of relational 'haunting' assemblages that may occur at these haunted locations.

Today, archaeological work is beginning to penetrate into the 'haunting' world of these sites, a fieldwork not normally part of the traditional archaeological site, but within the expanded conception of an archaeology in and of the present (cf. Harrison 2011). A recent example of this is Buchanan and Skousen (2015), in which the "activities, flows, and dissemination of nonhuman entities, bodies, spirits, ideas, forces, and memories through time and space [occur] in various dimensions and scales" (Skousen and Buchanan 2015: 11). This follows ethnographic reports (cf. Gardner 1987) in which 'abandoned' regions and sites frequently remain inhabited by spirits.

Archaeologists talk of "transformission" (cf. Watteaux 2014), a material memory of places and things (that transform and transmit) traces of the past as material remains in the contemporary scene, and of the futures that follow. Watteaux's paper is the study of the "memory of the forms of landscapes because they are memory objects that are transmitted as they are transformed in the time-space". If material memory, in the form of traces and fragments of buildings, artifacts, and burials are transmitted, why not sensory elements?

This 'transformission' of multi-temporal presences of memory traces and fragments, creates a fluid, 'haunting' site. These are locations that are not finished evolving because of the continual conjoining, now including ghost hunting groups, public ghost hunts, and ghost and dark tourism, of old, new, and future materials, behaviors, technologies and their residues. The ensuing state of flux, between becoming present and the ephemerality of most present site occupations (including archaeological) adds to the uncanny atmosphere of these places.

An example of this is the *Maison du Mage Project* (Letesson and Jusseret (2017a; 2017b), an archaeological survey of contemporary artifact assemblages of an abandoned house in the village of Marsal, Lorraine, France. The site, "the House of the Wizard", a "must-see attraction…for locals, curious passersby, thrill seekers, ghost hunters, and the like" (Letesson and Jusseret 2017b: 79) has a colorful history: "the eerie story of the Mage and his wife, his fondness for occultism and oriental folklore, the mysterious disappearance of two of his children in the late 1960's, the unresolved court case and the eventual abandonment of the house" (Letesson and Jusseret 2017a: 2). The house has a "unique atmosphere of desolation and uncanniness impregnating its walls" (Ibid: 2). The survey of the site included a "detailed photographic coverage/documentation" in developing "systematic and innovative approaches to modern ruins in ways that can convey something of the 'unspeakable' to colleagues or a wider audience, and give relevant accounts of their architectural nature" (Letesson and Jusseret 2017: 80-81).

During a recent Theoretical Archaeology Group (TAG) conference, a conference at which I have spoken many times, at Syracuse University (May 2019), a number of approaches to abandoned places and sites of ruin, in which this multiplicity of presences occurs, including 'ghost hunting' and ghost lore, were presented. Among these:

- "Archaeology and Public Engagement with Abandoned Mental Asylums' (Sarah Bell, Brown University). In this paper, the "largely undocumented archaeology of the asylum and the dark tourism aspect of their current appeal lie many truths about the past of mental health care" was discussed;

- "Rediscovering Forgotten Burials under Church Floorsand" (Sanna Lipkin (University of Oulu), Titta Kallio-Seppa (University of Oulu), AnneMarie Tranberg, Tiina Vare, Erika Ruhl) in which the speakers discuss a number of stories about the belief in "church people", "the deceased who controlled the churches at night". They discussed what church burial tradition and "what part of this heritage still remains…as well as the stories we as archaeologists tell the audience of different ages from child to elderly";

- "The North Remembers…Something? Erosion of Place and Memory in Western Iceland"

(Sarah E. Hoffman, University of Buffalo). In this paper, she talked about how the Church of St. Nicholas on the island of Haffiaroarey fell through the ice in 1563, with all parishioners killed including the parish priest. They are many versions of the story, but in all "the island was not only abandoned but haunted by ghosts of the drowned and restless dead". Her paper discusses "the role of environmental changes" [and] a narrative that transforms from one of death and abandonment [including ghostly presence] to a practical response to environmental change.

In all of these papers, ghosts and/or ghost stories form part of the archaeological narrative, some associated with both past memory and present experience and materialization. In a similar vein, ghost stories are common in National Trust and English Heritage presentations of UK heritage sites (Hanks 2015: 50-53).

On a personal note, our preliminary survey work at Bacon's Castle, coming at the invitation of CPRI, and specifically Robert Bradley, is another example of the archaeological fieldwork (cited above) at a haunted site. Bacon's Castle (Surry County, Virginia) is a place where different layers of temporality and experience can coexist and be explored archaeologically. The materiality of such buildings as Bacon's Castle is produced through continuous social practice amid change and deposition. This includes not only architectural features and artifact assemblages associated with these features, but also contemporary paranormal investigation. These transformations leave signature traces, both material and sensory.

Though Bacon's Castle is located near to Virginia's 'Historic Triangle', and is home to some of the country's most visited (Williamsburg) and best studied historical landmarks (Jamestown), archaeological work there has been sporadic. Engagements have focused on its representative value as an 'elite' plantation house ("the oldest brick dwelling in North America", according to Preservation Virginia website), there has been given little consideration to the house itself and surrounding landscape as a 'living', lived-in space.

It is an ideal location to explore, through a 'ghost excavation', and has been explored extensively by CPRI and is considered 'haunted' by various layers of memory. Using an archaeological approach of the contemporary past, one that explores the 'afterlives' of buildings and ruins, a extensive 'ghost excavation' would help to illuminate the mutually constitutive character of the place, and the 'lived' experience of what remains, as remainders of past layers of occupational history, ones that still 'haunt' visitors.

A hybrid approach that stops <u>materially</u> with the secession of continuous human construction (a 'ruin'), but continues <u>sensorially </u>with ongoing post-human (ghostly) attachments to particular acts, situations, and habits that are still percolating this memory into the present is a punk para-normal approach of an archaeology in and of the present. Such a hybrid approach allows us, as in the examples cited above, a sense of historical variability (though within the modern era), and an attention to the way that emotion, both in the atmosphere of the sites themselves and what remains of material culture in the present, affords presence through things and spaces.

This hybrid approach goes beyond contemporary archaeological tropes (and archaeology as ghost hunting; 'evil' archaeology), and the paranormal approach of ghost hunting. It also goes beyond the 'ghosts of place' suggested by Beisaw (2016a; 2016b). It is an engaged, immersive, and relational interaction between performance, memory, and the past (cf. Roach 1996). This model of fieldwork is meant to let go of the claims of 'authority', by ghost hunters, over 'what' and 'who' haunts a site, and the fieldwork process of physical excavation by archaeologists. This research is not a finished product, as are these haunted locations. Both are stages in the process of becoming present and being used as new fieldwork methodologies at these 'perceived' haunted locations.

Fieldwork becomes as much a reading of materiality still present and a reading from what still manifests sensorially to that materiality, both present and that which is now absent physically or in complete ruination. It is para-normal because it goes beyond the tropes of a 'normative' archaeology and beyond 'normal' ghost hunting., with its ghost tech saturations of space.

It has been suggested (Burstrom 2017), that the archaeological, as opposed to a historical, approach to the presence of this contemporary past memory in the present, involves a "need to be more attentive to how things affect us and to the emotions they evoke in our minds" (2017:221). I propose that it is this affect, coming from the past and retained in memory, that causes a haunting to occur. It is the result of how certain situations, events, beliefs, even habits in spaces surrounded by 'things' that leave 'signature 'traces' of both residual ('embedded') and interactive ('attached') presence. And it is the emotion of seeing and exploring buildings in ruin (and absence presence) that causes the perception of a possible haunting in ghost hunting.

The 'afterlife' effect of a perceived haunting, from an archaeological perspective, requires a context, and performance practices that 'target' that context, as a space-situation (event; habit) effect-resonating field practice, not a contemporary ghost tech scan or tech scan activation. This would allow us to distinguish a particular 'human' ('ghostly') effect (from the past) from other 'thing' effects (environmental process, ghost tech residue, ghost tech 'vibrant' matter', its material composition, or contemporary 'ghost hunting' emotional effect).

It is this potential 'affording' effect (through context-specific performances), rather that assuming a site's haunted nature based on a prior 'para-history', that should be the baseline of investigative practices, and from this baseline the questions that should be asked (rather than the arbitrary 'ghost hunting': "Is anyone here with us tonight?"). Using this 'archaeological gaze' to ascertain the existence (or not) of this (past) haunting effect is to acknowledge multi-temporal layers of embedded and attached 'memory presence': what was, what transformed, what now materializes as present.

This is continuity (or a 'haunting') at a site, perdurance, not 'para-history,' an absence present still under certain conditions (such as context-specific resonating acts that 'recall' situations, events, or habits from the past). This is a specific site-response, not a general, uncanny 'thing' that is manifesting. It is not a measurement, a reading, or a ghost tech activation. It is a horizontal gaze in the present that warrants vertical exploration. This is the archaeological sensibility (and sensitivity), punctuated by the possibility of still present layers of memory that continue to percolate in the present.

A haunting, in this archaeological sense, consisting of embedded or attached memories, is a space of 'embers': residues of 'heated' emotion, still containing a trace of life. When 'ignited' by practices that stir past experience, these memories can burst back into renewed presence, if only for some lingering moments.

Context-specific spatial practices that match past ones, I propose, are the 'fuel' for these haunting embers of memory to re-ignite and, in the process, can illuminate the 'identity' of past occupants at a site. Memory is the means by which a haunting is practiced in the present, a 'scripted' materialization. This memory, as a haunting register, is always bound up with place, space, practices, and experiences.

These layers of memory become fieldwork operations in directions other than archaeology's main focus (material culture) or that of the paranormal (context-specific performances rather than ghost tech measurements, scans, or device activations). It is memory, sensorial rather than material. It is perdurance, rather than hauntingly paranormal because the memory is already there, embedded in the space but attached as sensorial memory, not the 'ghost in the (contemporary) machine'. It is not beyond the 'normal', and is not 'para-history'. It is punk para-normal, an 'other' type of fieldwork within an archaeology in and of the present.

All haunting is contemporary haunting, what persists as past memory in the present. It is this perdurance of traces of emotional memory, attached to the past, or embedded in past layers, that still percolate in the present. The issue here is the <u>quality</u> of the manifestation, not the <u>quantity</u> of what manifests, its measurement or activation by an electronic device. This focus on quality has the potential of transforming the social organization of practices at haunted locations from a 'mash pit' of acts in a public 'ghost hunt' to a more concise way of seeing and listening, as a direct 'witness', rather than viewing and hearing through technological means.

It's time to make interpretations at the edge of performances in the field, with a quick response time during context-specific acts, targeting specific layers of potential embedded and attached memories. Analysis and response at the 'moment' of actualization is critical, not during post-field analysis, with the potential of both tech manipulation and memory loss.

The non-fragmentation of diverse data from multiple spaces at a haunted location is also essential. We must not think of haunted space as simply a puzzle, fitting together extraneous pieces of data that construct one's perception of a haunting. We must think, instead, of assembly-work, the simultaneous interaction of various 'actants' (agencies), processes, and effects all related: an assemblage (not an 'assembly line' of disparate 'bits' of data) of 'entities, objects, spaces, memories, sensorial elements, as a particular layer of past presence.

PUNK PARA-NORMAL: SPACE/SITE-SPECIFIC PERFORMANCE

"We begin as participants, rather than excavators" (Graves-Brown et al. 2013: 16).

Gregory Bateson (1972) has pioneered the ways in which sociocultural knowledge is both patterned and made present by forms of mediated acts. The question is: Does this sociocultural patterning (as possible perceived and recorded sensorial materializations at haunted locations) represent extensions past the original situation, event, and experience into the present? Do they become present again through contemporary context-specific performance practices at these supposed haunted locations?

Any distance between past and present, and that 'social distance' between investigator and a 'haunting' presence, can be overcome by allowing archaeologists, like myself, to challenge their own traditional archaeological tropes, and to explore, at these 'haunted' locations, the possibilities and unique opportunities of a creatively-engaged contemporary 'punk para-normal archaeology'.

Space/site-specific performance practices at haunted

locations can communicate, I propose, a cultural specificity within which particular sensory manifestations become meaningful. This is ethnographic texture: shaping behavior in such a way that makes it meaningful (and appropriate) in relation to the culture (the potential social layer of embedded memory) under investigation.

Through performance, the investigator becomes an actor. One learns and performs a role appropriate to the social context that is being 'excavated'. This is archaeology as a specific immersive excavation; excavation as performance practice. It is not archaeology as ghost hunting, or ghost hunting as archaeology. These performance practices can also be improvisational, but in a manner consistent and appropriate to the cultural context one is attempting to 'excavate'. This demands concentration on both the performance role, as well as those involved in observer roles.

This changes the role of fieldwork from a ghost hunt (or paranormal investigation) to an ethnographic immersion, rather than a reenactment of 'para-history'. It also changes the behavioral practices of the investigative team to a willingness to immerse themselves in both ethnographic detail and archaeological sensibility.

Morris (2018), in her practice-led PhD thesis, "interrogates the concept of inspirited landscapes in an Australian context. This 'inspirited landscape', according to Morris, was first coined by Peter Read (2003), who argued that time present and time past are inscribed on the Australian landscape in a matter that 'haunts'. According to

Read, "spirit sites may take the form of a soul or essence, be within the earth, be created by rites of passage or transformation, or be within archetypal mythologies drawn from East or West" (2003: 34). He further states that inspirited places receive and impart imprints as part of a process by which "spiritual forces…grow from the association between person and place" (Ibid: 255).

Inspirited, according to Morris, refers to the spirit of a site that may be enlivened by invoking the memories and histories that lay embedded in its layers" (2018: 4). She uses two site-specific projects "to create…'affective encounters' to demonstrate how historical affect and cultural memory flow through bodies, singular subjects and the places that are made transactive by the newly activated relationships" (Ibid: 4).

This is an example of intra-action, the relationality of assemblages that bridge time, between past and present. However, her approach is about "practices and social engagement through material aspects of site" (2018: 5). Her claim is that the Australian landscape "is inspirited with all that has been and replete with beings and becomings…[and] how site-specific creative practice can open our awareness and provide modes of engagement and potentially, modes of access…" (2018: 5).

This is similar to punk para-normal archaeology I am suggesting here. In contrast, however, though similarly working with context-specific material artifacts left behind at the site, I also include sensory 'cues' (such as sound and smell) to engage connection and intra-action between what remains (potentially) attached to the location and performance practices that may afford access to sensory memories of situations and events of past 'taskscapes'.

This ethnographic sensitivity changes the character of the manifestation from a 'ghost' (or worse, a non-human) to a cultural being with memory. It instills a basic humanness that replaces a paranormal event, or a 'portal to hell' and demonic possession. At a haunted site, many scenarios are possible, and these differ both with regards to a particular site's social stratigraphy, and the place and time (temporality) in which the haunting was first established, and how it becomes 'played out' in the present.

The performance practices, according to Morris (2018) act as "affective attunements and [the] registering of imperceptible affects that can point to points of connection and common experiences" (2018: 29). Can these 'common experiences' be an activation of experiences in past 'taskcapes'? Is this affecting past memories (perhaps attached and still 'active') being affective today as 'haunting phenomena': the 'active' presence of the past in the present?

Does this 'haunting' constitute an affective field, a relationality of past acts and contemporary performance practices as this haunting phenomenon bundle? Does this indicate that "human (and even non-human) activity…remain inherent and embedded as traces… and… it is possible to 'enact', re-perform and materialize these traces" (Morris 2018: 29) in the present, perceived as haunting phenomenon?

This is looking at a haunting, not as a universal typology of ghostly presences or even types of haunted sites, but rather with an emphasis "on the local, the specific, the particular, [that this] performance [space/site-specific] may provide as a means of indicating …how we are ourselves creating" (Pearson 2012: 67) a specific 'haunting' record.

What happens to a 'haunted' site, then, when what is brought there in the present creates a 'ghostly presence', 'things' and behaviors that were not part of the site's past biographical record? Could it be that ghost hunting, as it is practiced today, creates the trauma for any attached past presences, rather than past traumas creating the embedded ghostly presence? This reverses the paranormal belief that ghosts remain because of past traumatic events: do they <u>still</u> remain because of the 'trauma' created by today's ghost hunting acts and technologies?

In ghost hunting, this contemporary 'inspirited' haunted nature forms as anomalous manifestations, registering on ghost tech devices, as EVP recordings of "get out" (perhaps an indication of the creation of this ghost hunting 'trauma'). In archaeology, it is the unearthing, through excavation, of 'uncanny' artifacts or contexts. But in a punk para-normal archaeology, it is embedded/attached localized practices, signature cultural traces, sensorial memories of performances in past (continuing) 'taskscapes', a 'deep(er) mapping' of surfacing phenomena, that becomes a site's haunted nature. This deeper immersion becomes acts of 'place-making' at these sites, rather than re-enactments of known histories (much of which may not have anything to do with trauma). It also means that this place-making 'haunting', once bound to the specific place and its people and history, may be becoming, more and more, a 'normal' direct result of 'ghost hunting trauma, especially at 'paranormal hotspots'.

Performance, experience, and sensitivity to traces of memory, both past and present, are a triumvirate of relational inter-sociability during fieldwork that underscores how the past becoming present cannot be separated from contemporary re-occupations, meaning from sensuous re-habitation in punk para-normal fieldwork or in 'ghost hunting trauma'. This connection speaks to notions of presence and memory, and the fluidity of time, space, and performance that is a punk para-normal approach, and what may be happening through this 'ghost hunting trauma'. We need "response-ability" in two temporal spaces at a haunted location: the presence of past to present; resonating investigative practices in the present to penetrate the experiences and memories of the past. This 'ability' is achieved, I propose, through space/site-specific performances, not contemporary ghost hunting.

A 'performance' excavation of a site, using space/site-specific practices, is not destructive as is a physical excavation, or as traumatic as much of ghost hunting. One can 'target' lower (earlier) layers of potential embedded (to particular material artifacts/structures) or (sensorially) attached (to specific tasks/spaces) presences without erasing or suppressing those memories above or below that particular 'targeted' memory (of time and cultural expression). This does not mean, however, that one will not 'unearth' other manifestations of memory from these other layers of presence in the process .

This can occur as other presences of sensorial memory (especially visual and auditory) may manifest during the 'excavation' process. After all, a site is a location of continuing 'becomings', palimpsestual sweeps of new inscriptions and old erasures, as stronger fields of memory (habitual acts such as contemporary 'ghost hunts') can erase (or suppress) older memories, becoming new inscriptions.

This is what occurred during our 'excavation' of remaining battlefield presence at Burnside Bridge on the Antietam Battlefield (near Sharpsburg, Maryland, USA), where the single bloodiest day of combat in American history was fought on September 17, 1862. While taking photographs at the bridge entrance (from the Union assault side) at 1:00 a.m., a 'jogger in shorts' was photographed, but was not seen with the naked eye. He was not physically there, and this was confirmed by the NPS Ranger who was there with us.

Does this 'jogger' habitually jog this path, the scene of an 'avenue of approach' toward the objective (Burnside Bridge) by a number of Union assaults in the 1862 battle? Does (or did) his habit of jogging there, along this historical assault route, suppress past memory, described in historical narratives as a horrific scene of the dead and wounded, blood and body parts? That the jogging did not resonate with the movement of soldiers, and the emotional memory of those assaults, may be confirmed by the new imprint of casual jogging that became imprinted on the landscape there.

Does this indicate that non-space/site-specific performance practices erases past memories of presence? I propose that it does, and that is why a 'ghost hunt', with different behaviors and technologies brought to the site, can suppress or erase the embedded/attached presence of the past (and its 'ghosts') at these 'haunted' locations. Instead, ghost hunting frequently creates new 'ghosts', the contemporary 'live' ghost hunt. We have documented this process at other haunted locations, including Ft. Mifflin, near Philadelphia, Pennsylvania (USA). There, we recorded on the ground in the artillery shed, a series of K-2 meters, visually activated, yet none of us on the 'excavation' had a K-2 meter. We recorded, I propose, a previous 'ghost hunt' that used K-2 meters, producing a new, contemporary imprint upon the landscape of the historic fort.

Eviatar Zerubavel, in *Time Maps* (2003), refers to a "constancy of place". Establishing this 'constancy of place' is achieved by providing a physical location with "mnemonic bridging" (2003: 40-43), various strategies that create a sense of historical continuity, one that "allows us to virtually 'see' the people who once occupied the space we do now". A space/site performance, at a haunted location, can achieve this 'constancy of place' that can, I propose, 'unearth' those presences from the past who remain 'attached' to a particular space/place as 'ghosts'.

Fowler (2013) has said this: *"certain properties instilled in the assemblage during its formation [*I would include a 'haunting' as a particular assemblage] *out of these relationships endure as long as it enjoys some of the same relationships with certain forces, substances, entities, and so on as it currently does"* (2013:28). Space/site-specific performances are important acts at a haunted location. They, I propose, not only reinforce haunting manifestations, they allow it to endure through time. This can serve as a way to 'preserve' a haunting as a form of cultural heritage. In contrast, the possible 'trauma' created by ghost hunting results, I propose, in many hours of no activity occurring at the site. Instead, many times ghost hunters simply wait for something to happen.

To reiterate, the basic fieldwork operation in a punk para-normal approach is the space/site-specific performance. Its basic premise is to afford a particular form of communication between past and present, and between ghost and investigator. This form of communication is a resonance back to specific socio-cultural experiences and memories, not just habits of repetition that periodically (and ephemerally) are perceived to manifest at haunted locations. These socio-cultural manifestations are critical.

Waskul (2016), in his sample of individuals who have said that they have experienced a 'ghost', 68% of the descriptions lacked any human characteristics (2016: 139), let alone socio-cultural ones, context-specific to the various occupational layers of a site. Thus, "the reality of ghosts is essentially the result of an interpretation that…is greatly influenced by the stock of collective representations [of ghosts] internalized as facts" (Force 2018: 27).

Waskul (2016) states that those who have reported ghosts test their experience against folk theories, examine the available data, thus reducing possible explanations that eventually end as their (personal) ghost story (2016: 52). These representations of ghosts come from, I propose, the "cultural authority" (Hufford 1995: 18) of ghost hunters themselves through paranormal TV programming and social media. Zerubavel (2015) argues that people routinely ignore vast amounts of stimuli in the act of perceiving what [they]…are *taught is relevant* by one's social groups, principally the ghost hunting para-community

.

A punk para-normal approach is meant to 'unearth' a particular cultural being from the past with specific experiences and memories of their cultural world, not the world of 'ghost hunting'. Interactions between ghost and investigator is not so much cultural competence, as it is communicative competence (within past cultural worlds). It is by designing space/site-specific communicative (cultural) performance practices that directly relate to particular past layers of experience and memory that enable a perceived (or recorded) manifestation to be deemed culturally significant.

A punk para-normal approach is an attempt to expose particular cultural behaviors, usually hidden in ghost hunting activities (such as asking simple questions; ghost tech scans; the monitoring of empty, dark spaces), and are not general habitual acts, endlessly repeated through time and space. It is communicating in a particular socio-cultural way, and the observation/recording of responses that are resonant to that particular location's biographical landscape record. As an archaeologist, I undertake "research via field studies [at haunted locations] for the purpose of knowledge-making [that] is at one and the same time an observer and a participant" (Brown 2016: 20).

Space/site-specific performances work within unusual, provocative spaces to 'unearth' alternative layers of the reality of a haunted location. If affords the presence of the past to become present through specific tasks and practices, and the presence of material culture that is part of the archaeological record of the site. The integration of specific performance practices and material culture create, I propose, "two levels of analysis that do not contradict each other…We have objects that interact with each other…[and] we see the establishment of intentional relations among subjects [the presences of the past] and objects' (Ribeiro 2018: 5).

Two recent examples of site-specific performance, as a form of "theatre/Archaeology" (Pearson and Shanks 2001), are Costa and Ripanti (2013) and Theo and Kopaka (2019). Costa and Ripanti, in their excavation of the Roman mansion of Vignale (Italy) site offered "another way of approaching the excavation" (2013:97). They conceived "the site as a stage and digging as a performance" (Ibid: 97). This took the form of a communicative strategy between archaeological site and the public.

The archaeologists "acted at the site as if they were at the theatre, in order to invoke a wider public…[and] to make more understandable a very poorly preserved site…[as well as] make the work of archaeologists more clear" (2013: 100). They used the site as "the acting stage while the main characters are the archaeologists, who perform" (Ibid: 100). In the play, "archaeologists are part of the site as much as the remains…every area where archaeologists work can be considered as a sort of micro-acting stage" (2013: 104).

The performances involved, among other things, storytelling in which they stressed "what we tell is not 'what we have found' but 'what we are doing', favoring narration over interpretation" (Ibid: 106). This became an outline of the processes through which they reconstructed narratives of the past, which differs from the storytelling of 'para-histories' by ghost hunters. It is an example of situating the archaeological fieldwork, and the subsequent media produced, as a means of mediation and engagement with the public (Shanks 2007: 274).

In the paper by Theou and Kopaka (2019), a theatrical performance between archaeologists and actors was presented at Katalymata on the island of Gavdos off the coast of Crete. The performance was "based on the accounts in the excavation notebooks of the prehistoric activities revealed in the building's stratigraphy and enlivened by the memories of the modern islanders" (2019: 1286). What was different in this performance was the "extremely close relationship of its creative process with archaeological practice and research" (Ibid: 1289).

The focus of the performances was "the concept of

'house'", both in terms of past occupations as an archaeological site and the present as 'inhabited' by its excavators (and their actions who are shaping and suggesting narratives for the past following the material evidence that they uncover, but who are also drawing upon their own/personal embodied and cognitive experiences" (2019: 1290). This follows the suggestion of anthropologist Tim Ingold (2000) who states that "the practice of archaeology is itself a form of dwelling" (20000: 189-190). This type of 'theatre/archaeology' recalls Christopher Tilley's (1989) observation that " excavation has a unique role to play as a theatre where people may be able to produce their own pasts which are meaningful to them" (1989: 280)

However, a punk para-normal approach, as space/site-specific performance practices advocated in this book, differs in that it is concerned with how past_ peoples created their own presents, and how that experience may still remain embedded in contemporary 'perceived' haunted locations as fields of memory (as both residue in space and/or attached to objects still present in the contemporary environment, or becoming present through physical excavations). The 'audience' that is 'targeted' is not the contemporary public. Rather, the focus of communication in a punk para-normal approach is directed toward the 'ghosts' who may remain attached to the site, its spaces, or its material culture, that which remains present today. Both embedded residue and attached 'active' presence, I propose, at contemporary ruins and abandoned buildings are sensed (and recorded) sensorial 'artifacts' of past 'taskscapes' and/or habitual acts.

Space/site-specific performance practices, in the form of a punk para-normal approach, can become a 'learning theater' through 'ethno-archaeological acting', a venture that goes beyond a participatory re-enactment (as 'representing' the past) to include the observation of that acting producing it, and how it affects the presence of the past becoming present. This creates a different 'timescape' on the 'targeted' stage of particular memories where the past lies ahead.

This can 'manifest' the layers of memory through performance, and the impact of this on the perceptions of the investigator-observer, in 'working with' what has remained unnoticed previously. It is meant to document how performance and embedded/attached traces of the past can be linked to particular manifestations in the present.

This becomes an attempt to solve the puzzle of how certain remains, albeit sensory ones, of the past in the present 'normally' go unnoticed. It is because the solution many times is not technological scanning, monitoring, or 'observing' device activation. It centers on performance practices that, by simply using a ghost tech device, becomes a pre-programming for solutions about a haunting, not an answer. It is simply not 'communicating'.

In haunted space, fieldwork is meant to invoke intentional action. This is complicated by the fact that 'host' and 'ghost' are interchangeable as subject and object of an investigation, depending upon who acts intentionally to the other. The 'host' can be the investigator (in space-specific scenarios), who intentionally acts to make the 'ghost' manifest. The question is this: does the 'ghost' as this 'subject' intentionally manifest to the investigator (now the 'object' of attention)?

In a 'ghost hunt', this situation is different. The 'object' in the investigation is, in many instances, an environmental deviation, as a measurement of space (and not the 'ghost' as 'subject'). The ghost tech device becomes the 'host', which to past presence, is a 'ghost', something brought to the 'host' site, and which is not part of the experience and memory of the 'ghost'. In most 'ghost hunts', especially large public events, the 'investigator' is passive, while 'ghost tech devices' ('objects') become the 'subject' of intentionality.

A punk para-normal, on the other hand, embraces scenography, as a process within a sensual layer of embedded/attached memory, that becomes a central disciplinary method (cf. Hegel et al. 2019). This is a "focus on problem-setting and problem-setting to the design and staging of encounters with and among various publics" (Hegel et al. 2019: 4). It is working with (the 'audience') what remains of the past in the present as sensual layers of presence ('ghosts') at 'host' sites ('haunted' sites).

Performances, in various scenes of encounters, become synodochic (partial) points of re-occupying a haunted site within a particular layer of past memory. This scenography is a sensitivity to trace, residuality, fragmentation, and ephemerality of past presence becoming present. It sets in motion a sensuous discovery during non-evasive 'excavations' of particular (potential) haunted spaces at a site.

These potential encounters, as designed practices that are context-specific to particular sensual and emotional layers of embedded/attached memories (as situational and/or eventful past experience), shifts fieldwork towards "an embodied multi-modal co-constructed ethnographic experience...by the receptive engagement of its direct witness" (Ibid: 4), the 'ghost'.

This expanded immersion into haunted space occurs at the point of encounter in the field, and concerns social forms and connections (not 'objects' or measurements) of 'thick description' and "deep mapping" that can "create opportunities for embodied and participatory meaning-making about the emergent real" (Hegel et al. 2019: 5), the sensual presence of the past in the present (as a 'haunting'). Such an approach does not rely on "fixed measurement strategies" (as in ghost hunting), or quantifying differences and changes in ambient atmospheres. Rather, it seeks sublime, emotional webs of materializing presence as they connect to the enacted scenes of a space/site-specific performance.

This sensibility to possible sensual encounters has its roots in the concept of 'para-ethnography' through or enframing ethnographic encounters (Marcus 2000), and in site-specific performance (Pearson and Shanks 2001) as a connection between 'host' (a haunted site) and 'ghost' (the investigative team'). The 'aimed' result is a "dialogical cross-reconstruction of a given social context" (Kester 2004: 95) that still 'haunts' a particular place. It is meant to expand and 'deepen' our understanding of past social life that remains in the present at a haunted location, those presences that remain attached to particular social situations, specific events, or habitual acts. These relate to surfacing layers of presence relative to material objects, physical environment, and fields of memory.

One should always remember that the present 'normally' becomes the 'haunted' location because the past, as 'host', was a different cultural world. As Lucas (2001) has said, what "we dig… up…become something different because they enter a new cultural system" (2001: 142), the present. Let's make that present a little more 'accommodating' to what remains of the presence of the past. In a space/site-specific performance at haunted locations, we attempt to maintain that resonance as transition (not transformation) of that (those) past worlds into the present.

IT'S THE 'SURFACING' THAT COUNTS: 'HAUNTINGS' AS RELATIONAL MANIFESTATIONS

What is needed in the exploration and investigation of haunted sites is in-depth 'excavations' that take into account 'surfacing' manifestations that become present, not those presences presumed to exist and to be already there. This is not about past residue, but a concern for intra-action, a relational association between site biography, past experience and memory, and contemporary, context-specific performance practices.

If a haunted site (any site) is a series of horizontally-embedded layers where life has been lived at a particular time and place (cf. Simonetti 2018), then what manifests as haunting phenomena is a becoming present from these layers of embedded and attached presence. The surfacing of a haunting can be considered, I propose, as a sensing orientation toward *'minding'* and *'mattering'* in constant becoming (cf. Simonetti and Ingold 2018).

What matters is the connection between a continuing consciousness and its memory of its surroundings (space), the material culture in these surroundings, and the actions and tasks (as particular 'taskscapes') that were (are) performed there. To understand the meaning of a haunting is to understand these connections, a relationality between various elements in space and time.

The concept of relationality has increasingly become important in archaeology. In relational thinking, what things are and what they do is situational (and I would include haunting phenomena). This situational perspective relates to modes of being in the world, which differs from many assumptions of contemporary thinking (especially 'laws' characteristic of Western thinking and its mechanistic understanding of the world).

Relationality is about connections and entanglements. Making connections is also about openness, a sense of becoming present. It is not matter or process engulfed within rigid frameworks of typologies, or certain ways of doing things, like the tech-oriented ghost hunt, or even the archaeological trope of vertical, physical excavation. It assumes that reality is not bounded with clearly-defined parameters, linear temporalities, or binary thinking (such as past/present; subject/object; absence/presence; to name a few).

In relational thinking, non-humans (the environment and animals) have personhood and agency. There are other systems that operate in reality other than rationalism, and that constitute a form of knowledge production in particular cultural contexts. One aspect of relational thinking is "perspectivism" (Viveiros de Castro 1998). It suggests that different beings know the world from their own embodied perspective, such as different animals, because they both differ from humans and from each other in terms of different sensory apparatuses, different cognitions, different ways of interacting in the world and moving about.

A 'ghost', from a 'haunting perspectivism', is similar, I propose. It's 'afterlife' is different from the contemporary because it retains its own perspective of interacting in the world (different emphasis on sensory modes; ways of communication, etc.), while the world has changed, especially the technological world, and its newer extensions of perception and communication.

In relational thinking, culture and environment co-generate one another. A haunting represents a different 'perspective' than that of the present, and hauntings in different environments and different cultures also represent a different perspective. There is no universal typology of hauntings, haunted sites, or types of ghosts from a 'perspectivist' point of view. That is why context in an investigation, 'targeting' specific relationalities of cultural and environmental 'perspectivism' becomes important in documenting a 'ghost' becoming present.

In relational thinking, nothing is stable and fixed. Environmental measurements and scans, so common in ghost hunting, become dubious fieldwork exercises. So is doing the same thing at every haunted site. This forms a barrier to communication. It prevents interaction. It disallows the <u>normal</u> state of potential constant becoming, based on ongoing relational connectivity. That is why a haunting is situational. Context is important, typologies are irrelevant.

This requires continuous and active attentiveness to fieldwork practices at each site investigated. Each must be different, from that particular site's perspective and relational connections. This calls for adaptations to particular situations, based on site ethno-history, and not its 'para-history'. This permits site intra-action, it allows for a perspective of communicative competence.

The entanglement into a particular haunting phenomena is not 'in' things (tech devices), but 'between' them, in practices that follow the connections of a haunting assemblage: by making the relational connection with past experience (and thus memory) through the perspective of context-specific practices to what may remain 'embedded' (as residue) or 'attached' (as intra-active) of this assemblage, connections that remain as sensorial elements that relate to past occupational 'taskscapes' at the site.

A relationality in fieldwork, as its counterpart, a relationality in haunting phenomena, becomes a process or exchange of similar actions (as 'intra-action') that can afford what remains of the past in the present to become present. This is a stimulus to act, not a command (or request) to 'appear, or a 'response' to a unproven ghost tech device, which is *not*, in the majority of haunted locations, part of the relational connections to past experience and memory.

This is attending to surfacing phenomena as "transformative thresholds which manifest different qualities in the meeting of minds, bodies, materials, and earth" (Anusas and Simonetti 2020: 3), a relational haunting assemblage from the past that is afforded presence through specific space/site-specific practices that target a particular past layer of memory and experience of a particular 'taskscape', rather than some horrific event or uncanny past situation that most ghost hunters feels binds particular entities to particular locations.

This different approach centers on an ongoing process in fieldwork at haunted locations as an "education of attention" (Gibson 1986:254) to these potential connections to 'surfacing' manifestations. It is thinking about the relational aspects of a 'haunting assemblage', its intra-action between past experience/memory and present performance practices. Within this intra-action, one documents the flows, movements, and becomings that come from each contemporary performance practice.

It is one means to trace the continuity of 'remains' of past actions, other than what materially remains in the present, as in the traditional trope of archaeological excavation. These other 'remainders', as both sensorial residues and/or intra-active manifestations, continuing actions of past 'taskscapes', requires a different form of 'excavation' (a 'performative' rather than a physical one), and a different way to document a haunting, other than 'ghost hunting', as traces of these memories becoming present.

As philosopher Henri Bergson (1998) has said:

"wherever anything lies, there is, open somewhere, a register in which time is being inscribed…The very basis of conscious existence is memory…the prolongation of the past into the present, or that is to say duration acting…" (1998: 16-17).

Haunted sites are zones of transformation, acts of becoming present. They are not fixed within typologies, forms of presence (types of 'ghosts'), particular environmental measurements or readings, or physical laws. These sites are in a constant state of becoming: inscription, suppression, and erasures are constant processes there, depending upon the amount, intensity, and quality of contemporary non-resonating (not based on past experience, tasks, and habit memories) activities there.

In this type of fieldwork, we are more concerned in what this 'surfacing' of presence does (and how it relates to past 'taskscapes' and experiences), than what these manifestations are effecting, with regard to environmental changes. This 'excavation' approach, in contrast to its archaeological norm, the vertical unearthing of past material culture, is seen as a sensorial movement upward toward the surface and becoming present. In archaeological excavation, that movement is downward, except in an archaeology in and of the present, where past material (rather than sensorial) usually exists on the surface (cf. Harrison 2011).

In archaeology, the study of past presence is usually done "by moving in gravitational environments where things are supposed to fall and accumulate vertically, while the ground affords both horizontal locomotion and downward excavation (Simonetti 2018: 15). In archaeological excavation, this, according to Simonetti (2018), becomes the "capacity to *feel forward* …a movement not only towards the future, but also into the deeply buried past" (2018: 15). So, "as archaeologists move forward (downward) into the future…they also move forward into the past" (Ibid: 15).

In contrast, a space/site-specific contextual punk para-normal excavation uses practices , through resonance, to 'lift-up' the past (its 'ghostly presences' as sensorial elements) upward and become present today. This 'punk' approach also differs from an archaeology in and of the present which surveys the surface for physical, material remains. In ghost hunting, there is no 'digging' (either physically or performatively) into the past. That makes a punk para-normal approach both different from 'normal' archaeological tropes *and* 'normal' ghost hunting fieldwork.

Excavation in archaeology "emerges as a double vertical movement of downward destruction and upward reconstruction" (Simonetti 2018:16). In contrast a punk para-normal performance 'excavation' is neither destructive because it does not physically destroy the layers of past presence above the excavation grid, and the surroundings of the excavation zone. It is also not a re-construction. It does not inscribe new architectural features upon the ruin. It is also, with respect to ghost hunting, not socially destructive. It does not inscribe new behaviors onto the site. It is also not socially reconstructive. It does not inscribe new 'thing' elements (as haunting presence) based on ghost tech scans, activations, and environmental measurements.

A haunted site or, more specifically a haunted landscape, is a 'deathscape'. Described by Maddrell and Sidaway (2010), this is "both the place associated with the dead and for the dead, and how these are imbued with meanings…" (2010: 4-5). I am using this definition to go beyond the normal locations of bodily interment, the cemetery, to also include the places 'haunted' by the dead who remain attached to these places.

In their book, Maddrell and Sidaway (2010), in a collection of articles, show in various ways that 'deathscapes' are sites of place-making, of actions in which individuals actively act with material objects which enable them to (re)-introduce the dead into the social world of the living (cf. Wojtkowiak and Venbrux 2010). Does ghost hunting re-introduce 'ghosts' into the contemporary world through the use of ghost tech devices?

In these collection of articles, there is an examination of spaces involved in memory work, and the connections and relationships that the living have with the dead. These 'deathscapes' are relational assemblages of remembrance. All the essays included in the book identify acts that work towards assembling these deathscapes. Ghost hunting, in most of its diverse applications (such as the assumed 'scientific' paranormal investigation) act not to assemble, but to disassemble the 'deathscape' by changing remembrance at these places associated with the dead to 'edutainment' at best.

Ghost hunters do use a relational approach in fieldwork.

According to Hanks (2016), "they attend closely to their senses, chronicling any sounds, sights, unusual feelings, sensations, or thoughts that they experience" (2016: 264). This relational 'toolbox', however, is, for the most part, without past cultural context, not aligned to a location's biography of 'taskscapes', or even relative to the investigator's own actions that might have 'triggered' or afforded the manifestation in the first place.

These 'tools' (including the use of ghost tech devices and other technologies) do not "highlight the 'tools' objectivity and minimize their subjectivity" (Ibid: 265). The 'evidence' gathered from these 'tools' is assumed by ghost hunters "to speak for itself" (Hanks 2016: 265), which is "producing objective knowledge [which] simply requires describing the evidence accurately" (Ibid: 266).

In her Ph.D. dissertation, Hanks (2011) studied how ghost hunters attempt to produce legitimate knowledge at haunted locations through a mastery of these tools. In her dissertation, she notes the obstacles in converting these tools into evidential data and the "fantasy and suspicion that science [using these tools] can and should explain the entirety of the world" (2011: 361). This is scientism, not scientific fieldwork on the part of the ghost hunter.

What is missing in the ghost hunting analysis of the ghosts of past 'taskscapes' is context. Meaning of what remains (both archaeologically and 'ghostly') is bounded within contexts. The documentation and potential meanings of a haunting, I propose, is narrowed by these contexts: context includes its chronological context, its spatial context, and its association to sensory output that are associated with the 'taskscapes' that are part of the site's occupational history, rather than contemporary ghost tech scans and measurements that indicate deviations in various fields of environmental conditions.

Without a specific context in place, many abandoned buildings and sites become 'fonts' on which to portray small-scale dioramas, using discarded 'artifacts' to fill in storylines. Exploring the possibilities of these storylines,

"becomes an exercise in social archaeology. Each item presents a subjective narrative…a world between solid objects and imagined possibilities. Without human activity to define function and atmosphere, the building takes on its own shifting reality…invites us to romanticize, to find magic, mystery, and beauty, to weave our own realities around the space" (Samuels 2012).

This is the danger of an association between abandoned buildings/sites and non-context-specific descriptions. It affords imaginative conjectures, rather than context-based historical archaeological reality, thus altering the material memory of the place. Is it any wonder that these places become 'haunted' by ghost hunters?

Those who explore these sites (and perform there), apart from ghost hunters (such as artists, photographers, and urban explorers, to name a few), have the ability to decouple the scene. They can over-aestheticize what remains behind, and the spaces of their containment (cf. Pusca 2010).

Context is not a site's 'para-history'. It is situated in

localized social, spatial, and temporal parameters. These fields of memory were created and are retrieved, I propose, through participatory practices in these past 'taskscapes', using sensory cues, and associations of objects that are not part of the present. These are actions that perpetrate a sense of relationality to 'this happened here'. This type of history is performing something and in a way with objects outside the 'normal' experience of the contemporary every day, or the 'typical ghost hunting mode'.

It is not documenting the passage of time, through the observation and survey of ruin and decay (as in archaeology); nor through environmental scanning and measurements (as in paranormal investigation/ghost hunting). It is intra-actions, a particular patterned rhythm of situational, relational actions. The fields of haunting bundles, assembled from past 'taskscape' assemblages, are what the 'ghosts' still do, connected to tasks and situations that have extended beyond individual (or group) lifespans.

The rhythms of multiple, past 'taskscapes' have distinct sensory effects of purposive and transformative actions, such as particular 'soundmarks' that differ from the present. A human past 'taskscape' haunting, or fragments of it, is what is left behind when that particular taskscape is no longer 'animated' by 'tasking actions'. Much of contemporary human hauntings are sensory 'artifacts', the residues of context-specific taskscapes that are embedded in the landscape.

The actual 'ghost', as an interactive past human presence, is quite rare. It is one who remains and still performs within certain tasks, based on their experience and memory. These hauntings are more common on battlefields, such as those of the American Civil War (1861-1865). On these battlefields, perhaps thousands of soldiers still lie in unmarked graves, buried far from home, without being accorded the rituals of the 'good death'. They remained attached to their military 'taskscape', performances in battle (or 'Inherent Military Probability (I.M.P.) behaviors learned in drills). A similar haunting assemblage (military death in battle, burial away from home, non-completion of 'good death' ritual) occurs in Vietnam, a product of the U.S. Vietnam War era (1964-1975) (cf. Kwon 2008).

The question remains: Do objects, like ghost tech devices and environmental scanning devices (such as EMF meters), really matter to the dead (as 'haunting presences')? Do real human ghosts really 'manifest' to questions and commands by ghost hunters? Do they really use these devices to show their presence? Do the environmental scans, as part of the ghost hunting 'toolkit', really provide meaningful data that indicates a ghostly materialization is becoming present, or do these environmental readings indicate something else?

Killian Driscoll (2017) suggests that landscape itself can be considered as something like a performance. She views this as a continuing process that is never completed. Thus a landscape, upon which a haunted site is located, may be 'haunted' by what is called 'environmental performance' (cf. Lindelof et al. 2017), and not a ghostly human haunting presence. Environmental performances are environmental processes "offer experiences of time passing", a "continuous time-space unfolding in real-time" and "natural forces outside human control" (Lindelof et al. 2017: 229). Might not these processes be what ghost tech scans and measurements at haunted locations are detecting?

Environmental performance is a type of performance that focuses "on emergent environmental activity that is indeterminate…exceeding the…realm of socio-cultural interaction, communication and organization…Things change, move, and connect with other things without showing any sign of intention…" (Lindelof et al. 2017: 233). This is not ghostly, human presence.

These environmental performances become framed through the use of ghost tech devices, scans, and measurements. They then become reassembled and labeled as a haunting manifestation by 'ghosts'. The framing draws particular attention to a part of living, dynamic, and 'normal' environmental processes which ghost hunters do not separate from possible human haunting manifestations.

The use of devices, such as the video camera and the audio recorder are used "as a formal differentiation that isolates a part of the perceptual environment (the environmental performance] as a particular event" (Ibid: 234) which, I propose, becomes part of a site's 'para-history'. Thus, ghost hunting takes a normal assemblage of different environmental conditions and processes by which a location is produced and perceived as a 'haunted' site.

A good example of this environmental performance are

'audio atmospheres'. They are mysterious. As David Toop, in *Haunted Weather* (2004) says:

"Much of their content may be invisible…their cumulative effects come from elusive and under-researched phenomena such as pressure changes, infrasound, ultrasonics, and other barely perceived sonic signals aligned with subtle transitions in the acoustic environment…They are thick with imaginings, memories, utopias, foreboding" (2004: 54).

But they are not paranormal. These audio atmospheres are especially relevant in ghost hunting, when fieldwork is normally done at night. This is because "sounds do travel further at night…and man-made noise is also reduced" (Ibid: 53). Many ghost hunting recordings of EVP have another potential audio problem. They could be a form of "audio mirage", which "can emerge from prolonged listening to an identical recording where you almost begin to hear things not actually recorded" (Toop 2004: 85). Is there an "archaeology of [acoustical] loss" (Ibid: 86) 'unearthed' by ghost hunting EVP recordings, or are they simply environmental performances of audio atmospheres and/or 'audio mirage' on the part of the ghost hunter listening to their recordings at haunted sites over and over again until they detect distinct words or phrases?

Yet, environmental performances "are performative in the basic sense of the word because they 'act' environmentally and produce [normal] environmental effects" (Lindelof et al. 2017: 236). This performance and those effects have occurred throughout the history of the planet. That they are, at times, unpredictable and random, does not make them paranormal. Though they may have periods of time with more activity, more intensity, and 'elevated' affect, and at other times remain inactive, does not make their measurement on a ghost tech device a 'haunting'. Though these environmental performances become a 'live' relational event, they are not a human 'ghost' manifesting.

These perceptions ('paranormal', 'haunting', 'ghost') are due to a certain framing of particular sites by ghost hunters which "combines with a heightened awareness and response to the enframed world" (Ibid: 240) to produce these haunted locations. What is occurring at these locations, most times, is "emergent unpredictability" (Lindelof et al. 2017: 239) of these environmental performances.

One can use, however, material objects found at the haunted site as 'triggers', so long as they relate to past occupations of particular 'meshwork' bundles/assemblages. We have ourselves used, besides these context-specific objects, non-human elements (such as context-specific sounds and smells) on American Civil War battlefields in our 'excavations' at Antietam, Gettysburg, Monocacy, and other battlefield sites. We have also used environmental resonance, such as the time of year the battle was fought (summer, fall), rather than actual anniversary dates.

We do not use the ghost hunting typology of 'anniversary ghosts': "witnessing a ghostly presence on (or very close) to the date of a specific or corresponding event of significance to the ghost" (Waskul 2018: 65). According to Waskul (2018), these "are much more common in popular culture than everyday life, and people seem to expect anniversary ghosts…more often than they are actually experienced" (2018: 65). This is because 'leap years' change these dates. We rely on "environmental performance", as changes during particular times of the year, as a 'tool' to 'stimulate' a potential manifestation.

Questions remain: Are the dead (as 'ghosts') actively engaged in the way they are interacted with by the living? Is there a 'haunting assemblage' that permits agency and communication between spirits (popularly configured as 'ghosts') and the living? A recent paper "seeks a deeper and more nuanced understanding of the roles and agency of the dead and spirits. [It defines] and reconfigures the way we enable the dead to communicate with us…" (Heng 2020). In ghost hunting, the re-introduction to the contemporary world is not an uncanny form of remembrance. It is, in large measure on a ghost hunt, entertaining.

Heng (2020) offers a concept that encompasses the role of spirit interactions through material objects in 'assembling' these deathscapes. He finds its place in "material rather than surface geographies". In ghost hunting in Western cultures, are objects (ghost hunting devices) mediums through which ghosts can communicate with the living?

Heng (2020) uses the term "material proxies of consociation" as a "formal way of linking agency with the activeness of objects". Objects are significant in Chinese religion, and Heng's ethnographic study was done among Chinese religious practioners in Singapore. Heng uses the term 'proxy' for these objects to suggest more activity and engagement than a 'tool', referred by Hanks (2016) above, for the ghost hunter's use of ghost tech devices.

The use of 'consociation' means that the entity is " not just talking to individuals, it is actively interacting with them" (Heng 2020). Is this what happens on a ghost hunt? The spirits in Heng's study are 'ancestral souls', however, and ghost hunting, for the majority of cases, are not dealing with their past ancestors. So, the question remains: is there a relational connection between contemporary ghost tech devices, as 'tools', and perceived manifestations at a haunted location, when that assumed association is not based on past experiences and revived as memory to a ghost tech device? I think not. Perhaps, that is why many 'hunts' contain hours of inactivity, or even why batteries drain on devices? Is this an indicator of a 'lack of interest, a confused state, or even a sense of trauma on the part of the ghost?

The relationality of associations in haunting phenomena not only assemble a 'deathscape', they may also indicate the active role of ghosts in such assembling. The connection between practices, both past and present, as intra-actions in a haunting manifestation may be key. It is in this space of intra-action when that absence becoming present may work. This intra-action, I propose, is a 'haunting' manifestation in real time.

The relationality of intra-action creates contemporary

emotional effects that identity that space as haunted. This re-structures fieldwork at these sites. We do not need to use tech devices as ghost hunters do, as a saturation of space to support the idea that these ghost tech devices are the proper 'tools' to verify phenomena. This ethnographic study by Heng (2020) uses an approach that follows other contemporary methods, most notably participatory action research (O'Neill 2011) and video participatory methods (Bates 2014).

Ethnographic studies, such as those of Heng (2020) have shown that spirits have their own ways of influencing the outcome of a potential interaction with a 'live' human, rather than the reverse: the ghost hunter, through their ghost tech devices initiates contact. This is part of a new way of understanding how absence can remain at haunted locations and how this absence can be made present, especially when the investigator is using practices known to have been performed at the site, and remain as sensorial memories.

A haunting, becoming present, is a 'performance remain', an archaeological trace that becomes, through 'excavation' as space/site-specific performance practices, a form of 'audiencing' (observing) a past performance, experience, encounter, and liveness. It is not that the ghostly presence (be it visual, auditory, or olfactory) is 'live', but rather we still are, in the present, experiencing the sensorial becoming 'live'.

One more important question is this: what happens if two temporally distinct taskscapes occupy the same space (one a past haunting layer of presence; the other a contemporary haunting presence, the 'ghost hunt')? What 'presence effects' may result in this coupling? Are there new inscriptions, old erasures, or older 'haunting suppressions? If we are enacting context-specific performance practices, targeting a particular past layer of memory, and getting 'other' anomalies (not 'targeted'), might not these 'anomalies' be from other, past 'ghost hunts', rather than from other older (or more recent) layers of past presence becoming present? Might these ghost hunt anomalies be more frequent at paranormal 'hot spots': those sites frequently explored in large, public ghost hunts and/or frequent ghost tourism? No matter what is occurring (inscription , erasure, or suppression) of past 'human' haunting or contemporary past 'ghost hunting' residue, the reality of a haunted location is a 'mess'. And that is why we need a systematic, and controlled 'excavation' and analysis of these sites.

SUMMARY:
PUNK PARA-NORMAL ARCHAEOLOGY
NOT
ARCHAEOLOGICAL PUNK OR PUNK GHOST HUNTING

"Time's wheel runs back or stops:
Potter and clay endure"
• Robert Browning.

In ghost hunting, time's wheel stops: the past is present through technology, waiting to be measured and recorded. In archaeology, excavation exposes back ('peels away') what remains, in material trace and fragmented form, of the past in the present. In punk para-normal archaeology, contemporary performances resonate with those of the past, bringing forth (potentially) both 'human ghost' and sensorial memory' as it was in the past at the site, in the form of an ephemeral 'taskscape'.

The archaeology I explore at haunted sites, especially those abandoned buildings, sites, and landscapes, is this study of the sensorial memory of the past in the present, not the past itself revealed through material culture. It is not what archaeologist Laurent Olivier (2011) states is the 'normal' work of archaeology: the study of material memory. It aligns more with archaeologist Christopher Witmore (2015), who states that archaeology's concern is with "memories held within and between specific things" (2015: 383).

The loss of sensorial memory in the normative trope of archaeological excavation is worthy of attention. These 'ghosts' are not a form of absence, only absent in most archaeological fieldwork, as survey and excavation focus on what material culture and structures survive in the present. What is needed in the field at these haunted locations is a 'spirit' of para-normal performance-based experimentation. In this experiential fieldwork, we do not use technology to compensate for the absences inherent in what remains of past presence in the present ('haunting phenomena' in ghost hunting; material remains in archaeology).

This is because, I propose, it is the loss of sensory memory that is missing in both 'normative' ghost hunting and the documentation of a site's archaeological record, including those sites perceived to be haunted. In ghost hunting, it is the real loss of cultural presence relative to past situations and events in 'taskscapes', and that sensorial residue that may remain today from those performances. This is due to ghost hunters use (or overuse) of ghost tech devices, apps, and other technologies which may only be documenting 'normal' processes (environmental), agencies (contemporary human), and mechanisms (the internal composition of their tech devices).

In archaeology, with its focus on the archaeological, it is exclusively centered on locating and recording, through survey, excavation, and technological means, both surface and hidden below surface remains of material culture. It is at a loss to record and document potential 'surfacing' sensory 'artifact' assemblages of past relational bundles of performance practices in various 'taskscapes'.

The concept of the 'archaeological' in archaeology is an acknowledgement of these potential surfacing sensorial artifact assemblages as absences. They do not exist as something 'archaeological', and thus do not 'haunt' descriptions of the archaeological record, even at abandoned sites and ruins. Their absence is not loss (through site formation processes) because they are not considered 'archaeological'.

This creates a problem in the biographical record of sites, including potential 'haunted' locations. There is a "logical gap" (Polanyi 1958) between two frames of mind: the ghost hunting 'paranormal' and archaeology's 'archaeological': one (ghost hunting) may be misrepresenting most claims to 'haunting phenomenon' because they are not recording real 'losses', replacing them with absences becoming presences as 'things' (environmental anomalies), not past human cultural behaviors.

This 'loss' is being recorded through unproven ghost tech devices, and other tech scans. These recordings, scans, and measurements, for the most part, may be merely recording 'normal' environmental processes and other (other than human cultural 'ghostly') agencies and mechanisms. This indicates that ghost hunting may only be one form of a site formation process which transforms abandoned sites and ruins into a perceived haunted location. This is a result of ghost tech inscriptions onto the landscape, a misinterpretation of 'natural' environmental processes, human agency, material residue as haunting phenomena, and recordings (both video and audio) on social media without context-specific accompanying narratives by untrained observers of natural-occurring phenomena.

The other (archaeology) is not 'normally' interested, in these types of fieldwork operations, the documentation (or even existence) of 'ghosts' and 'hauntings' because they are considered 'absences' (not 'losses'): they don't form part of the 'archaeological', the traces and fragments of material culture. What remains of material culture in the present is already a 'loss' from the transformations through time of original 'material memory', or complete past 'taskscapes', due to various site formation processes through time.

Thus, what has not been there (a 'ghost' in archaeology), or did not become sensed (most of the time in ghost hunting without ghost tech aid) may be there and present, but not as a ghost in the 'normal' paranormal sense, but as sensorial memory: past acts of situations/events of 'taskscapes' that still occupy spaces of abandonment and ruin in residue form.

Both fieldwork operations at abandoned building sites and ruins ('normal' ghost hunting and archaeology) are "relying on the framework of interpretation [thus] cannot demonstrate a proposition to persons who rely on *another* framework" (Polanyi 1958: 151, emphasis in original). Thus, ghost hunting is not archaeology; archaeology is not ghost hunting because, principally, they treat the ideas of loss and absence differently.

Both neglect what a potential 'haunting' *is* because both assert what ghost hunting and archaeology *are*. Both confuse, I propose, the difference between the condition of absence and the contingency of loss. This is due to the difficulty in both to acknowledge the reality of 'otherness' because it represents a condition different from what ghost tech devices represent and what material culture suggests. The deficiency is compensated by eroding this 'otherness' by making it 'paranormal' (a normal absence registered present by ghost tech devices), or saying it is not archaeological (a normal 'loss' verified by material trace and fragmentation).

This converts the data within both frameworks to something else: 'thing' anomalies in ghost hunting, or something familiar, material culture in archaeology. Instead of a more complete inventory and understanding of what remains at these sites, the presence of the past is literally only accessible through ghost tech devices and other 'normal' hunting practices (such as asking questions; monitoring space); or through the archaeological, material fragmented/trace remains as material memories of the past.

A site record, even a 'haunted site's record, I propose, is cultural phenomena that remains 'static' in the present (not adapts to technological changes as in ghost hunting), and has no people (only material cultural traces/fragments in archaeology). Because of this predicament, the issue of 'ghosts' becoming present, and the status of a site being haunted, cannot be addressed from within these two existing (normal) frameworks. Again, archaeology is not ghost hunting, and ghost hunting is not archaeology. And both have limited capacities, in their own ways, to document a 'ghost' and 'haunting phenomena'.

The solution lies in the concept of 'para', something beyond 'normal' ghost hunting and archaeology. One way to approach this differently is a punk para-normal archaeology: something beyond the normality of standard operating fieldwork in both ghost hunting and archaeology; and beyond the 'usual suspects' of the 'ghost in the machine', the 'haunting' moments of discovery during archaeological excavation, and the possible 'vibrant matter' of material memory.

What we need is thicker, richly-detailed descriptions of what becomes present during fieldwork: the overlooked (or ignored) sensorial cultural becomings that 'thickens' a remembrance of those experiences that may still remain embedded/attached to past 'taskscapes' in spaces at a site. In doing this, a deeper mapping of conflicting sensorial temporalities can enliven reports and prevent misshapen productions of the 'place-making' of haunted locations.

This necessity for a 'thick' description is especially

relevant at abandoned building and sites of ruin because what is left visually may not be all the remainders that remain of past occupations. At these locations, perception and sense are out of place because what remains is seen as messy and unorganized. There is no relational integrity that is perceived at these sites because there is a sense of decay and ruination.

There becomes a need to re-organize the present by the 'unearthing' of any continuing relational integrity that may still be continuing at these sites, amid all the mess, traces, fragments, and processes of physical and cultural ruination. This is where a punk para-normal archaeology comes in. It is the time in fieldwork that can, I propose, re-surface fieldwork to something beyond the 'normality' of 'execution habituality' that is characteristic of 'normal' ghost hunting and archaeology.

Thus, it is the manner in which ghost hunters and archaeologists normally express their work, so detached from that unique cultural encounter with sensorial memory. This alienates both from something beyond their 'normal' fieldwork encounters. It is the loss, many times, of wonder in fieldwork because it is framed as a conformity to normal patterns of acceptable fieldwork activities. It makes sense to follow that 'habit memory' of conformity, rather than becoming a 'punk' and being para-normal.

There is thus a need for a reconfiguration of fieldwork practices at these abandoned buildings and sites of ruin for a different way toward knowledge production. Neill Whitehead (2009) has argued that "it is only through active participation that there is anything to observe at all" (2009: 5). We must make our observations at haunted locations become linked to participatory practices that create a context-specific relationality between participation and what is then observed. This is "observant participation" (Ibid: 5), a performative and radical participation and its observation. This is 'punk', the ethnography of alternative fieldwork that is inspired by archaeology as 'performance excavations'.

Being 'punk', as one reconfiguration, can afford particular (and different) "presence effects" (Gumbrecht 2004), beyond the accepted normal. This involves a sense of the presence of the past in the present. This presence sense is, however, not the normal sense of experiencing a 'ghost'. The focus of Gumbrecht (2004), for example, is on emergence and experience at, I propose, the edge of meaning: what and how, in the case of a haunting, potential haunting phenomenon manifests. I suggest that data on hauntings, and their meaning (as space/site-specific) can be revealed by direct experience, an intra-action encounter in a relational connection between past sensorial memory and contemporary space/site-specific cultural contextual practices, a 'performance excavation'. This is being 'punk', as something different from both ghost hunting and archaeology.

Being 'punk' is a view of a haunting presence that is not absent. It is there, embedded and/or attached in or to a site, in specific spaces. The haunting is not discontinuous from its past relational entanglement. It is not a misinterpretation or the 'ghost in the machine'. It is not abandonment in contemporary abandoned places. It persists. It is there. The question centers around how to make it become present. That is punk para-normal archaeology, through contextual space/site-specific cultural performance practices.

To forget or ignore the relational connection between past imprinting and today's manifestation, common in both ghost hunting and archaeology, does not work (or is a meaningful subtraction). As Gibson (2002) has said, "Wishful amnesia is no protection against memories of actual, lived experience. The events of the past rarely pass. They leave marks in documents, in bodies, in communities and places, in buildings, streets and landscapes" (Gibson 2002: 179). The question of how to connect with these haunting memories, as relational assemblages, must be preceded by the question of how to behave at these sites of ruin, and abandoned buildings. It is how to observe, and how to respond when the haunting becomes present again in the present.

Making connections to embedded/attached sensorial (and behavioral) memory is a re-focus from a visual survey of ruination to a para-normal archaeology that expands the archaeology beyond the accustomed role of archaeologists. It is making sense of what sensorially remains in trace and fragmented forms (or the ghost hunter's making sense of 'anomalies' through their ghost tech devices). Let's be 'punk', open ourselves to include 'affect', sensation, emotion, and 'uncanny' experiences, even when those experiences may point to an uncanny 'other', the sensory experience that is 'out of place' which now can matter too.

<u>Note:</u>

A recent book (to be published May 2020) may be a change in archaeological thinking. This book, *Blurring Timescapes, Subverting Erasures: Remembering Ghosts on the Margins of History* (Sarah Surface-Evans, Amanda E. Garrison, and Kista Supernant (Editors), Berghahn Books) is described "as a book that demonstrates the value of conceiving of ghosts not just as metaphors, but as mechanisms for making the past more concrete…".

According to one review, it "represents contemporary archaeological praxis that realigns the possibilities of archaeological theory through radical, brave, and at times vulnerable intersectional standpoints that inform a new way forward…" Uzma Z. Rizvi, Pratt Institute).

APPENDIX: SPACE/SITE-SPECIFIC PERFORMANCE 'EXCAVATIONS'

A. References in My Books:

1. *Bodies of Substance, Fragments of Memories: An Archaeological Sensitivity to Ghostly Presence* (2009)

- "A Prolonged Childhood: The Yuengling Mansion Hauntings" (Pottsville, Pennsylvania). pp. 51-57.
- "The Jeremy Haunting" (Gettysburg, Pennsylvania). pp. 58-64.
- "Cultural and Non-Verbal Communication at Eastern State Penitentiary" (Philadelphia, Pennsylvania). pp. 87-133.
- "The Petersburg Civil War Battlefield" (Petersburg, Virginia). pp. 114-136.
- "The Continuing Presence of the 15th Alabama at Little Round Top" (Gettysburg, Pennsylvania). pp. 137-174.

2. *Beyond the Paranormal: Learning from the Past at Haunted Locations* (2013)

- "The Knick in Time" (The Knickerbocker Hotel, Linesville, Pennsylvania). pp. 95-124.
- "Haunted Centers of Learning" (The Brunswick

Railroad Museum, Brunswick, Maryland). pp. 167-188.

3. _The Production of Haunted Space: It's Meaning and Excavation_ (2013)

- "The 'Signs' of Presence in Haunted Battlefield Space" (Antietam Battlefield, Sharpsburg, Maryland). pp. 78-106.

4. _Digging Up Ghosts: Unearthing Past Presences at a Haunted Location_ (2013)

- "Beyond the Darkness: A Memory Practice into the World of William Howe" (Ft. Mifflin, Philadelphia, Pennsylvania). pp. 288-297.

- "The Rohrbach (Burnside) Bridge Ghost Excavation" (Antietam Battlefield, Sharpsburg, Maryland). pp. 298-380.

5. _An Archaeology without Borders: Performance Excavations in Embedded/Entangled Fields_ (2016)

- "The Contemporary Burnside Bridge Entangled Haunted Network" (Antietam Battlefield, Sharpsburg, Maryland). pp. 187-206.

B. Conference Talks (see Academia.edu/John Sabol)
(Access is free)

- "The Seen, Unseen, and the Non-Sensed(d): 'Excavating Victorians at the Bedford Springs Resort and Spa" (Bedford, Pennsylvania).

- "Sensual Archaeologies: The 'Second Reality' of an Historic 'Warscape' Setting" (Antietam Battlefield, Sharpsburg, Maryland).
- "Dark Peripatetic Engagements: An Ambulation through Experience and Memory in a Landscape of Destruction" (Centralia, Pennsylvania).
- "Centralia, Pennsylvania: The Multiple Entanglements of Layers of Memory"
- "The Strange 'Nightlife' of an (Otherwise) Serious Archaeologist: An Emotional 'Excavation' of Serious Strange Experiences" (various locations).
- "Hanover Tavern, Virginia: 'Animating' the Historical Landscape- Principles of Interaction with Architecture and its Attached Ghosts through a Site-Specific 'Performance Excavation'".
- "The Gettysburg 'Memoryscapes' of War: Layers of Spiritualist Absence and Ghostly Presence in the Heterotopia of a 'Haunted' Battlefield".
- "A 'Ghost Town' without a Town: Multiple Entanglements in the Centralia Landscape" (Centralia, Pennsylvania).

BIBLIOGRAPHY

Abrams, David. 2018. Magic and the Machine: Notes on Technology and Animism in an Age of Ecological Wipeout. *Emergence Magazine,* Issue 3.

Ackroyd, Peter. 2011. *The English Ghost: Spectres Through Time.* Vintage Books.

Alberti, Benjamin. 2016. Archaeologies of Ontology. *Annual Review of Anthropology* 45 (1): 163-79.

Anusas, Mike and C. Simonetti. 2020. Introduction: Turning to Surfaces in *Surfaces: Transformations of Body, Materials, and Earth.* Edited by Mike Anusas and C. Simonetti. London: Routledge. pp. 1-13.

Arnold, Bettina. 1999. The Contested Past. *Anthropology Today* 15 (4): 1-4.

Baires, Sarah E., Amanda J. Butler, B. Jacob Skousen, and Timothy R. Pauketat. 2013. Fields of Movement in the Ancient Woodlands of North America in *Archaeology After Interpretation.* Benjamin Alberti, Andrew M. Jones, and Joshua Pollard (Editors). Walnut Creek, California: Left Coast Press. pp. 197-218.

Barth, Theodor. 2019. Introduction: Exposition and Transposition- Seeking an Ontologic Sensoriality in Contingencies in *Artistic Practices and Archaeological Research.* Dragos Gheorghiu and Theodor Barth (Editors). Oxford:

Archaeopress Publishers LTD. pp. 1-12.

Bates, C. 2014. *Video Methods: Social Science Research in Motion*. London: Routledge.

Bateson, Gregory. 1972. *Steps to an Ecology of Mind*. Chicago: University of Chicago Press.

Beer, David. 2014. *Punk Sociology*. New York: St. Martin's Press.

Beisaw, April M. 2016a. DRAFT Paper prepared for "Haunted Landscapes" Session of SHA.

2016b. Ghost Hunting as Archaeology, Archaeology as Ghost Hunting in *Lost City, Found Pyramid: Understanding Alternative Archaeologies and Pseudoscientific Practices*. Edited by Jeb J. Card and David S. Anderson. Tuscaloosa: University of Alabama Press. pp. 185-198.

Bennett, Jane. 2001. *The Enchantment of Modern Life: Attachments, Crossings, and Ethics*. Princeton: Princeton University Press.

2010. *Vibrant Matter: A Political Ecology of Things*. Durham: Duke University Press.

Bergson, Henri. 1998. *Creative Evolution*. New York: Dover Mitchell.

Bierwert, Crisca. 1999. *Brushed by Cedar, Living by the River: Coast Salish Figures of Power*. Tucson: University of Arizona Press.

Bosco, Rocco. 2018. Ghost Archaeology: Heritage of a Haunted Continent in *Defining the Fringe of Contemporary Australian Archaeology: Pyramidiots, Paranoia, and the Paranormal*. Darran Jordan and Rocco Bosco (Editors). Newcastle upon Tyne, U.K: Cambridge Scholars Press. pp.

33-46.

Brittain, Marcus W.R.   2013.   Assembling Bodies, Making Worlds: An Archaeological Topology of Place in *Archaeology After Interpretation*. Benjamin Alberti, Andrew M. Jones, and Joshua Pollard (Editors). Walnut Creek, California: Left Coast Press. pp. 257-276.

Brown, Steve.   2016.   Experiencing Place: An Auto-Ethnography of Digging and Belonging. *Public Historical Review* Volume 23: 9-24.

Bryant, Levi R.   2014.   *Onto-Cartography: An Ontology of Machines and Media.* Edinburgh: Edinburgh University Press L+D.

Bubandt, Nils.   2019.   Spirits as Technology: Tech-Gnosis and the Ambivalent Politics of the Invisible in Indonesia. *Contemporary Islam* 13: 103-120.

Buchanan, Meghan E. and B. Jacob Skousen (editors). 2015. *Tracing the Relational: The Archaeology of Worlds, Spirits, and Temporalities.* Salt Lake City: University of Utah Press.

Caraher, William.   2014. *Punk Archaeology.* Edited by William Caraher, Kostis Kourelis, and Andrew Reinhard. University of North Dakota: Digital Press.

2015. *Slow Archaeology.* North Dakota Quarterly. Volume 80.2

Chumley, Lily Hope and Nicholas Harkness.   2013. Introduction: Qualia. *Anthropological Theory* 13 (1/2): 3-11.

Clarke, Philip.   2007.   Indigenous Spirit and the Folklore of Settled Australia. *Folklore* 118: 141-161.

Costa, Stefano and Francesco Ripanti.   2013. Excava©tion   in   Vignale: Archaeology   on   Stage,

Archaeology on the Web. *Online Journal in Public Archaeology*. Volume 3: 97-109.

Course, Magnus. 2007. Death, Biography, and the Mapuche Person. *Ethnos* 72 (1): 77-101.

Cruikshank, Julie. 2005. *Do Glaciers Listen? Local Knowledge, Colonial Encounters, and Social Imagination.* Vancouver: UBC Press.

Cunningham, Jerimy J. and Scott MacEachern. 2016. Ethnoarchaeology as Slow Science. *World Archaeology*. Volume 48, Issue 5: 628-641

Davis, Eric. 2015. *TechGnosis: Myth, Magic and Mysticism in the Age of Information.* Berkeley: North Atlantic Books.

Dawdy, Sharon. 2010. Clockpunk Anthropology and the Ruins of Modernity.

2019. Death and Archaeology in the Present in *Rethinking Historical Time: New Approaches to Presentism.* Edited by Marek Tamm and Laurent Olivier. London: Bloomsbury Academic. pp. 179-191.

Deloria, Philip J. 2006. What is the Middle Ground Anyway? *The William and Mary Quarterly* 63 (1): 15-22.

Dolar, Mladen. 1999. I Shall Be with You on Your Wedding Night: Lacan and the Uncanny. *October* 58: 5-23.

Driscoll, Killian. 2017. Approaching the Mesolithic through Taskscapes: A Case Study from Western Ireland in *Forms of Dwelling: 20 Years of Taskscapes in Archaeology.* Edited by Ulla Rajala and Philip Mills. Oxford: Oxbow Books.

Edensor, T. 2005. *Industrial Ruins: Space, Aesthetics, and Materiality.* New York: Berg.

Espirito-Santo. 2019. Spectral Technologies, Sonic

Mobility, and the Paranormal in Chile. *Ethnography* 0 (0): 1-20.

Figal, Gerald. 1999. *Civilization and Monsters: Spirits of Modernity in Meiji Japan.* Durham: Duke University Press.

Fish, Stanley. 1980. Is There a Text in This Class? The Authority of Interpretive Communities. Cambridge: Harvard University Press.

Force, William Ryan. 2018. Toward a CryptoScience in *The Supernatural in Society, Culture, and History.* Edited by Dennis Waskul and Marc Eaton. Philadelphia: Temple University Press. pp. 18-34.

Fowler, Chris. 2016. Relational Personhood Revisited. *Cambridge Archaeological Journal* 26 (3): 397-412.

Fowler, Chris. 2013. *The Emergent Past: A Relational Realist Archaeology of Early Bronze Age Mortuary Practices.* Oxford: Oxford University Press.

Foxhall, L. 2012. Material Values: Emotion and Materiality in Ancient Greece. In *The Role of Emotions in Ancient Greece.* A. Chaniotis, P. Ducrey. Stuggart: Steiner .

Fredengren, C. 2016. Unexpected Encounters with Deep Time Enchantment: Bog Bodies, Crannogs, and 'Otherworldly' Sites. *World Archaeology* 48: 482-499.

Gabry, Jennifer. 2011. *Digital Rubbish: A Natural History of Electronics.* Ann Arbor: University of Michigan Press.

Gardner, D.S. 1987. Spirits and Conceptions of Agency among the Mianmin of Papua New Guinea. *Oceania* 57: 161-177.

Gell, Alfred. 1998. *Art and Agency Anthropological Theory.* Oxford: Clarendon.

Gibson, James J. 1986. *The Ecological Approach to Visual Perception.* Hillsdale, N.J: Lawrence Eribaum Associates.

Gibson, Ross. 2002. *Seven Versions of an Australian Badland.* St. Lucia: University ofQueensland Press.

Gonzalez-Tennant, Edward. 2016. Hate Sits in Places: Folk Knowledge and the Power of Place in Rosewood, Florida in *Excavating Memory: Material Cultural Approaches to Sites of Remembering and Forgetting.* Edited by Maria T. Starzmann & John R. Roby. University Press of Florida. pp. 218-241.

Gosden, C. 2004. Aesthetics, Intelligence and Emotions: Implications for Archaeology. in *Rethinking Materiality: The Engagement of Mind with the Material World.* E. De Marrais, C. Gosden, C. Renfrew (Editors). Cambridge, UK: McDonald Institute Monogram. pp. 33-42.

Govan, 2007. Between Routes and Roots: Performance, Place, and Diaspora pp. 136-143.

Grady, Jill C. 2011. Ancestors, Ethnohistorical Practice, and the Authentication of Native Place and Past in *Phantom Past and Indigenous Presence* Edited by Colleen E. Boyd and Coll Thrust. Lincoln: University of Nebraska Press. pp. 280-300.

Graves-Brown, P., Rodney Harrison, and Angela Piccini. 2013. Introduction in *The Oxford Handbook of the Archaeology of the Contemporary World.* P. Graves-Brown, R. Harrison, and A. Piccini (Editors). Oxford: Oxford University Press. pp. 1-26.

Green, Miranda A., 2004. *An Archaeology of Images: Iconology and Cosmology in Iron Age and Roman Europe.* New

York: Routledge.

Gumbrecht, Hans U. 2004. *Production of Presence: What Meaning Cannot Convey.* Stanford: Stanford University Press.

Hahn, Hans Peter. 2008. Diffusionism, Appropriation, and Globalization: Some Remarks on Current Debates in Anthropology. *Anthropos* 103: 191-202.

Harvey, D. 1990. *The Condition of Postmodernity: An Enquiry into the Origins of Cultural Change.* Oxford: l.

Hegel, Christine, Luke Cantarella, and George E. Marcus. 2019. *Ethnographic Design: Scenographic Experiments in Fieldwork.* London: Bloomsbury Academic.

Hamilakis, Y. and A. Anagnostopoulos. 2009. What is Archaeological Ethnography? *Public Archaeology* 8: 65-87.

Hanks, Michele. 2011. Between Belief and Science: Paranormal Investigators and the Production of Ghostly Knowledge in Contemporary England. Ph.D. Dissertation,, University of Illinois, Urbaba-Champaign.

2015. *Haunted Heritage: The Cultural Politics of Ghost Tourism, Populism, and the Past.* Walnut Creek, California: Left Coast Press.

2016. Redefining Rationality: Paranormal Investigation Humour in England. *Ethnos* Volume 81, 2: 262-289.

Harman, Graham. 2005. *Guerilla Metaphysics: Phenomenology and the Carpentry of Things.* Chicago: Open Court.

2012. *The Quadruple Object.* Winchester, U.K: Zero Books.

Harrison, Rodney. 2011. Surface Assemblages: Toward an Archaeology *in* and *of* the Present. *Archaeological Dialogues*

18 (2): 141-161.

Harrison, Rodney and John Schofield. 2010. *After Modernity: Archaeological Approaches to the Contemporary Past.* Oxford: Oxford University Press.

Hay, Simon. 2011. *A History of the Modern British Ghost Story.* Basingstoke: Palgrave MacMillan.

Heng, Terence. 2020. Interacting with the Dead: Understanding the Role and Agency of Spirits in Assembling Deathscapes. *Social and Cultural Geography.*

Hodder, Ian. 2012. *Entangled: An Archaeology of the Relationships Between Humans and Things.* Oxford: Wiley-Blackwell.

Holtorf, Cornelius. 2008. Studying Archaeological Fieldwork in the Field: Views from Monte Polizzo in *Reading Archaeology: An Introduction.* Edited by Robert J. Muckle. Plymouth, U.K: Broadview Press. pp. 146-155.

2016. Are we all archaeologists now? Introduction. *Journal of Contemporary Archaeology* 2 (2): 217-219.

Houlbrook, C. 2013. Ritual, Recycling, and Recontextualization: Putting the Concealed Shoe into Context. *Cambridge Archaeological Journal* 23 (1): 99-112.

Huber, Sanda. 2019. Villains, Ghosts, and Roses or How to Speak with the Dead. *Open Cultural Studies* 3: 15-25.

Hufford, David. 1995. Beings Without Bodies: An Experience-Centered Theory of the Beliefs in Spirits in *Out of the Ordinary: Folklore and the Supernatural.* Edited by B. Walker. Logan: Utah State University Press. pp. 11-45.

Huhtamo, Erkki and Jussi Parikka (Editors). 2011. *Media Archaeology: Approaches, Applications, and Implications.*

Berkeley: University of California Press.

Ingold, Tim. 1993. The Temporality of the Landscape. *World Archaeology* Volume 25, No. 2: 152-174.

2000. *The Perception of the Environment: Essays on Livelihood, Dwelling, and Skill.* London: Routledge.

2007. *Lines: A Brief History.* Oxon: Routledge.

2011. *Being Alive: Essays on Movement, Knowledge, and Description.* London: Routledge.

Johnson, Matthew. 1999. *Archaeological Theory: An Introduction.* Oxford: Blackwell Publishing Ltd.

Jones, Andrew M., Benjamin Alberti, Christopher Fowler, Gavin Lucas. 2013. Archaeology After Interpretation in *Archaeology After Interpretation: Returning Materials to Archaeological Theory.* Benjamin Alberti, Andrew M. Jones, Joshua Pollard (Editors). Walnut Creek, Ca: Left Coast Press. pp. 15-35.

Kester, G.H. 2004. *Conversation Pieces: Community and Communication in Art.* Berkeley: University of California Press.

King, Stephen. 1982. *Danse Macabre.* London: Futura.

Kopytoff, Igor. 1986. The Cultural Biography of Things: Commoditization as Process in *The Social Life of Things: Commodities in Cultural Perspective.* Edited by Arjun Appadurai. Cambridge: Cambridge University Press. pp. 64-91.

Kundu, Amitava Michael. 2011. The Paradox of Contemporary Paranormal Research. http://soulsearchers.spheresoflight.com au/the paradox-of-contemporary-paranormal-research/2011. Accessed

1/31/2020.

Kwon, Heonik. 2008. *Ghosts of War in Vietnam.* Cambridge: Cambridge University Press.

Ladwig, Patrice. 2013. Ontology, Materiality, and Spectral Traces: Methodological Thoughts on Studying Lao Buddhist Festivals for Ghosts and Ancestral Spirits. *Anthropological Theory* 12 (4): 427-447.

Landrum, Cynthia. 2011. Shapeshifters, Ghosts, and Residual Power: An Examination of Northern Plains Spiritual Beliefs, Location, Objects, and Spiritual Colonialism in *Phantom Past, Indigenous Presence: Native Ghosts in North American Culture and History.* Edited by Colleen E. Boyd and Coll Thrush. Lincoln: University of Nebraska Press. pp.255-279.

Laqueur, Thomas W. 2015. *The Work of the Dead: A Cultural History of Mortal Remains.* Princeton, New Jersey: Princeton University Press.

Latour, Bruno. 1993. *We Have Never Been Modern.* C. Porter (Translation). London: Prentice-Hall.

2005. *Reassembling the Social: An Introduction to Actor Network Theory.* Oxford: Oxford University Press.

Letesson, Quentin and Simon Jusseret. 2017a. The *Maison du Mage Project:* Whay Remains for Archaeology? *Journal of Contemporary Archaeology* 4.1: 1-18.

2017b. The *Maison du Mage* Project: Surveying Contemporary Assemblages in *Clashes of Time: The Contemporary Past as a Challenge for Archaeology.* Edited y J.M. Blaising, J. Driesses, J-P Legendre, and L. Olivier. Paris: Presses Universitaires de Louvain.

Levi-Strauss, Claude. 1966. *The Savage Mind.* Oxford: Oxford University Press.

Lindelof, Anja, Ulrik Schmidt, and Connie Svabo. 2017. Environmental Performance: Framing Time in *Experiencing Liveness in Contemporary Performance: Interdisciplinary Perspectives.* Edited by Matthew Reason and A.M. Lindelof. Oxon: Routledge, Routledge Advances in Theatre and Performance Studies, Nr. 47. pp. 229-240.

Lorenz, Chris. 2010. Unstuck in Time, Or: The Sudden Presence of the Past in *Performing the Past: Memory, History, and Identity in Modern Europe.* Karin Tilmans, J. Winter (eds.). Amsterdam University Press. pp. 67-102.

Lucas, Gavin. 2001. Destruction and the Rhetoric of Excavation. *Norwegian Archaeological Review* 34 (1): 35-46.

2004. Modern Disturbances: On the Ambiguity of Archaeology. *MODERNISM/Modernity* 11 (1): 109-120.

2013. Afterword: Archaeology and the Science of New Objects in *Archaeology After Interpretation: Returning Materials to Archaeological Theory.* Benjamin Alberti, Andrew M. Jones, Joshua Pollard (Editors). Walnut Creek, California: Left Coast Press. pp. 369-380.

2015. Archaeology and Contemporaneity. *Archaeological Dialogues* 22 (1): 1-15.

Lynn, Heather. 2019. *Evil Archaeology: Demons, Possessiions, and Sinister Relics.* Newburyport, MA: Disinformation Books.

Maddrell, A. and J. D. Sidaway (Editors). 2010. *Deathscapes: Spaces for Death, Dying, Mourning and Remembrance.* Farnham: Ashgate.

Malpas, Jeff. 2012. *Heidegger and the Thinking of Place: Explorations in the Topology of Being.* Cambridge, MA: MIT Press.

Marcus, George E. 2000. *Para-Sites: A Casebook against Cynical Reason.* Chicago: University of Chicago Press.

Marshall, Y. 2009. Community Archaeology in *The Oxford Handbook of Archaeology.* C. Gosden, B. Cunliffe, B. Joyce (Editors). Oxford: Oxford University Press. pp. 1078-1102.

Maxwell, Robert. 2018. Collision Ahead: Non-Linear Time and the Elsewhen in *Defining the Fringe of Contemporary Australian Archaeology.* Darran Jordan and Rocco Bosco (Editors). Newcastle upon Tyne, U.K: Cambridge Scholars Press. pp. 136-144.

McLuhan, Marshal. 1964. *Understanding Media: The Extensions of Man.* London: Routledge.

Merleau-Ponty, M. 1962. *Phenomenology of Perception.* C. Smith (Translation). London: Routledge.

Meskell, Lynn. 2005. Archaeological Ethnography: Conversations around Kruger National Park. *Archaeologies* 1 (1): 81-100.

Miller, Daniel. 1987. *Material Culture and Mass Consumption.* Oxford: Basil Blackwell.

Mills, Barbara J. and William H. Walker (Editors). 2008. *Memory Work: Archaeologies of Material Practice.* Santa Fe: School for Advanced Research Press.

Moore, Lawrence E. 2013. *Trowel Love: Essays on the Sociology of American Archaeology.* Broken Arrow, Oklahoma.

Morgan, Colleen. 2012. *Emancipatory Digital Archaeology.*

Thesis, University of California (Berkeley).

2015. Punk, DIY, and Anarchy in Archaeological Thought and Practice. *Online Journal of Public Archaeology.*

Morris, Louis. 2018. Out of the Ruins: Australian Sites, Inspirited Landscapes and the Social Sacred. PhD Thesis: Deakin University.

Munn, N. 1986. *The Fame of Gawa: A Symbolic Study of Value Transformation in a Massim Society (Papua New Guinea).* Durham: Duke University Press.

Nativ, Assaf. 2017. No Compensation Needed: On Archaeology and the Archaeological. *Journal of Archaeological Method and Theory* 24: 659-675.

Olivier, Laurent. 2011. *The Dark Abyss of Time: Archaeology and Memory.* Lanham, Maryland: Altamira Press.

O'Neill, M. 2011. Models: Arts, Migration and Diaspora. *Crossings: Journal of Migration and Culture* 2 (1): 13-37.

Panagiolopoulos, A. and Diana Espirito Santo. 2019. Introduction in *Articulate Necrographies: Comparative Perspectives on the Voices and Silences of the Dead.* Edited by Panagiolopoulos A. and D. Espirito Santo. New York: Berghahn.

Parikka, Jussi. 2012. *What is Media Archaeology?* Cambridge: Polity Press.

2015. *A Geology of Media.* Minneapolis: University of Minnesota Press.

2019. Remain(s) Scattered in *Remain.* Ioana B. Jucan, Jussi Parikka, and Rebecca Schneider. Minneapolis: University of Minnesota Press. pp. 1-47.

Parkin, David. 1986. *The Anthropology of Evil.* Edited by David Parkin. Oxford: Basil Blackwell LTD. pp. 1-25.

Pauketat, Timothy. 2013. *An Archaeology of the Cosmos: Rethinking Agency and Religion in Ancient America.* London: Routledge.

2020. Introducing New Materialisms, Rethinking Ancient Urbanisms in *New Materialisms, Ancient Urbanisms.* Edited by Susan M. Alt and Timothy R. Pauketat. New York Routledge. pp. 1-18.

Pearson, Mike. 2006. *In Comes I: Performance, Memory, and Landscape.* Exeter: University of Exeter Press.

2012. Raindogs: Performing the City. *Cultural Geographies* Volume 19, No. 1: 67-68.

Pearson, Mike and Michael Shanks. 2001. *Theatre/Archaeology.* London: Routledge.

Perry, 2018. Building Archaeology without Recording. *Journal of Contemporary Archaeology* 4 (2): 213-220.

Peters, John Durham. 1999. *Speaking into the Air: A History of the Idea of Communication.* Chicago: University of Chicago Press.

Petursdottir, Dora. 2013. Concrete Matters: Ruins of Modernity and the Thing Called Heritage. *Journal of Social Archaeology* 13 (1): 31-53.

2014. Things out of Hand: The Aesthetics of Abandonment in *Ruin Memories: Materialities, Aesthetics and the Archaeology of the Recent Past.* Edited by Bjornar Olsen and Dora Petursdottir. London: Routledge.

Polanyi, M. 1958. *Personal Knowledge: Towards a Post-Critical Theory.* Chicago: University of Chicago Press.

Praetzellis, Adrian. 2003. *Dug to Death: A Tale of Archaeological Methodology and Mayhem.* Lanham: AltaMira Press.

Pusca, A. 2010. Industrial and Human Ruins of Postcommunist Europe. *Space and Culture* 13 (3): 239-255.

Read, Peter. 2003. *Haunted Earth.* Sydney: University of New South Wales.

Ribeiro, Artur. 2018. Death of the Passive Subject: Intentional Action and Narrative Explanation in Archaeological Studies. *History of the Human Sciences* pp. 1-17.

2019. Archaeology and the New Metaphysical Dogmas: Comments on Ontologies and Realities. *Forum Kritische Archaologie* 8: 25-38.

Roach, Joseph. 1996. *Cities of the Dead: Circum-Atlantic Performances.* New York: Columbia University Press.

Rosa, H. 2013. *Social Acceleration: A New Theory of Modernity.* New York: Columbia University Press.

Russell, I.A. and A. Cochrane (Editors). 2014. *Art and Archaeology: Collaborations, Conversations, Criticisms.* New York: Springer-Kluwer.

Sabol, John G. 2013. *Burnside Bridge: The Excavation of a Civil War Soundscape.* Brunswick, Maryland: Ghost Excavator Books, Inc.

2014. *The Good Death and the Civil War.* Brunswick, Maryland: Ghost Excavator Books, Inc.

2017. *Geographies of Memory/Landscapes of Ritual: The Excavation of Forgotten Battlefield Presence.* Bedford, Pa: Ghost Excavation Books, Inc.

Samuels, J. 2012. Fair Mile Asylum, online. www.milliondollaryack.com/ghoststations/archives/2008/03/17/fair_mile_asylum.

Schneider, Rebecca. 2019. Slough Media in *Remain*. Ioana B. Jucan, Jussi Parikka, and Rebecca Schneider. Minneapolis: University of Minnesota Press. pp. 49-107.

Sconce, Jeffrey. 2000. *Haunted Media: Electronic Presence from Telegraphy to Television*. Durham: Duke University Press.

Shanks, Michael. 1995. Archaeological Realities: Embodiment and a Critical Romanticism in M. Tusa and T. Kirkinen (Editors) The Archaeologist and their Reality: *Proceedings of the 4th Nordic TAG Conference,* Helsinki, Department of Archaeology.

2007a. Politics of Archaeological Leadership in *Archaeology and the Media*. Timothy Clack and Marcus Brittain (Editors). Walnut Creek: Left Coast Press. pp. 273-289.

2007b. The Archaeologist and the Artist meet up to talk about Presence. *Seed Magazine*. http://seedmagazine.com/content/article/Michael_Shanks _Lynn_Hershman_Leeson/.

Shanks, Michael and C. Tilley. 1992. *Reconstructing Archaeology*. London: Routledge.

Simonetti, Christian. 2014. Feeling Forward into the Past: Depths and Surfaces in Archaeology. *Time and Mind* pp. 1-21.

2018. *Sentient Conceptualizations: Feeling for Time in the Sciences of the Past*. Abingdon: Routledge.

Simonetti, Christian and Tim Ingold. 2018. Ice and

Concrete: Solid Fluids and Environmental Change. *Journal of Contemporary Archaeology* 5 (1): 21-33.

Skousen, B. Jacob and Meghan E. Buchanan. 2015. Introduction: Advancing an Archaeology of Movements and Relationships in *Tracing the Relational: The Archaeology of Worlds, Spirits, and Temporalities*. Edited by Meghan E. Buchanan and B. Jacob Skousen (Editors). Salt Lake City: University of Utah Press. pp. 1-20.

Smith, Andrew. 2010. *The Ghost Story 1840-1920: A Cultural History*. Manchester: Manchester University Press.

Soja, Edward W. 1996. *Thirdspace: Journeys to Los Angeles and Other Real-and-Imagined Places*. Cambridge: Blackwell.

Stearns, P.N. and C. Z. Stearns. 1985. Emotionology: Clarifying the History of Emotions and Emotional Standards. *American Historical Review* 90 (4): 813-836.

Stevens, Vanessa and Jeffrey A. Tolbert. 2018. Beyond Metaphorical Spectrality: For New Paranormal Geographies. *New Directions in Folklore* Vol. 16, No. 1: 27-57.

Stockhammer, Philipp W. 2020. Doing/Changing Things/Us in *Exploring Materiality and Connectivity in Anthropology and Beyond*. Edited by Philipp Schorch, Martin Saxer, Marlen Elders. London: UCL Press. pp. 36-50.

Suchman, Lucy A. 2007. *Human-Machine Reconfigurations: Plans and Situated Actions*. Cambridge: Cambridge University Press.

Sutin, Lawrence (Editor). 1995. *Philip K. Dick, The Shifting Realities of Philip K. Dick: Selected Literary and Philosophical Writings*. New York: Pantheon.

Taussig, Michael. 1987. *Shamanism, Colonialism, and the Wildman: A Study in Terror and Healing*. Chicago: University of Chicago Press.

1993. *Mimesis and Alterity: A Particular History of the Senses*. New York: Routledge.

Theou, Efthimis and Katerina Kopaka. 2019. 'Gavdos: The House'. A Theatre/Archaeology Narrative and Pieces of Knowledge of Diachronic Home Life. *Heritage* 2: 1286-1299.

Thomas, Antonia, Daniel Lee, Ursula Frederick, Carolyn White. 2017. Beyond Art/Archaeology: Research and Practice after the 'Creative Turn', Creative Archaeologies Forum. *Journal of Contemporary Archaeology* 4.2: 121-129.

Thrush, Coll. 2011. Hauntings as Histories: Indigenous Ghosts and the Urban Past in Seattle in *Phantom Past, Indigenous Presence: Native Ghosts in North American Culture and History*. Edited by Colleen E. Boyd and Coll Thrush. Lincoln: University of Nebraska Press. pp. 54-81.

Tilley, Christopher. 1989. Excavation as Theatre. *Antiquity* 63: 275-280.

Toop, David. 2004. *Haunted Weather: Music, Silence and Memory*. London: Mackays of Chatham.

VanDyke, Ruth M. and Reinhard Bernbeck (Editors). 2015. *Subjects and Narratives in Archaeology*. Boulder: University Press of Colorado.

Viveiros de Castro, Eduardo. 1998. Cosmological Deixis and Amerindian Perspectivism. *The Journal of the Royal Anthropological Institute* Volume 4, No. 3: 469-488.

Waldron, David and Sharn Waldron. 2019. Ghosts of

the Goldfields: Ballarat as a Haunted City. *Urban Spectrality* pp. 229-248.

Wallace, Jennifer. 2004. *Digging the Dirt: The Archaeological Imagination*. London: Gerald Duckworth & Co. Ltd.

Waskul, Dennis with Michele Waskul. 2016. *Ghostly Encounters: The Hauntings of Everyday Life*. Philadelphia: Temple University Press.

Waskul, Dennis. 2018. Ghosts and Hauntings: Genres, Forms, and Types in *The Supernatural in Society, Culture, and History*. Edited by Dennis Waskul and Marc Eaton. Philadelphia: Temple University Press. pp. 54-75.

Watteaux, Magali. 2014. Concepts and Methods for Exploring the Forms of Landscape in the Long Term: The Case of French Archaeography. EAA Conference Paper, Istanbul.

Weidman, A. 2014. Anthropology and Voice. *Annual Review of Anthropology* 43: 37-51.

Whitehead, Neill. 2009. Post-Human Anthropology. *Identities: Global Studies in Culture and Power* 16(1): 1-32.

Wise, J.M. 2011. Assemblage in C. J. Stivale (Editor). *Gilles Deleuze: Key Concepts*. Durham: Acumen. Pp. 91-102.

Witmore, Christopher. 2015. No Past but Within Things in *Allegory of the Cave Painting*. M. Mircan and V.W.J. van Gerven Oei (Editors). Antwerpen: Extra City Kunsthal. pp. 375-394.

Wojtkowiak, J. and E. Venbrux. 2010. Private Spaces for the Dead: Remembrance and Continuing Relationships at Home Memorials in the Netherlands in a. Maddrell and

J.D. Sidaway (Editors) *Deathscapes: Spaces for Death, Dying, Mourning and Remembrance.* Farnham: Ashgate. pp. 207-221.

Zedeno, Maria Nieves. 2013. Methodological and Analytical Challenges in Relational Archaeology: A View from the Hunting Ground in *Relational Archaeologies: Humans, Animals, Things.* Edited by Christopher Watts. New York: Routledge. pp. 117-134.

Zerubavel, Eviatar. 2003. *Time Maps: Memory and the Social Shape of the Past.* Chicago: University of Chicago Press.

2015. *Hidden in Plain Sight: The Social Structure of Irrelevance.* Oxford: Oxford University Press.

ABOUT THE AUTHOR

John Sabol is an archaeologist, cultural anthropologist, actor, and author. As an archaeologist, he has unearthed past material remains in excavations and site surveys in England, Mexico, and at various sites in the United States (including Eastern South Dakota, the Tennessee River Valleys, and in Pennsylvania). His anthropological fieldwork includes the studies of "spirits" in the religious beliefs of the afterlife among various cultural groups in Mexico (Mixtec, Zapotec, Lacandon, Nahuatl, and Otomi). His acting career includes "ghosting" performances of various characters and scenarios in more than 35 movies, TV shows, and documentaries. He has appeared in the A&E TV series, Paranormal State as an investigative consultant.

His recent speaking engagements include the T.A.G. (Theoretical Archaeology Group) Conference at the University of California, Berkeley, at the Space and Place Conference in Prague, Czech Republic, the TAG Conference at the University in Buffalo, New York, Exploring the Extraordinary Conference in York, England, the C.H.A.T. archaeological conference also in York, and the GHost Conference at the University of London,

London, England.

His investigative reports have been published in such diverse venues as Haunted Times Magazine, Tennessee Anthropologist, and the online journal, ParaAnthropology. He has been a frequent guest on numerous radio and internet talk shows, among them, Beyond the Edge Radio, The Paranormal View, Para X Radio, Blog Talk Radio, The Grand Dark Conspiracy, and Rusty O'Nhiall's "Mysterious and Unexplained" on PsiFM (Australia). He was a university professor in Mexico for 11 years, teaching both undergraduate and graduate courses on the anthropology of tourism. He has also been featured on public educational TV for U.S. and foreign markets, and has worked on international educational documentaries (in Spain).

He has a M.A. in Anthropology/Archaeology (University of Tennessee), and a B.A. in Sociology/Anthropology (Bloomsburg University). He has also attended Penn State University, the University of Pittsburgh, the University of the Americas (Cholula, Puebla, Mexico), and has studied theatre and method acting in Mexico City.

He can be reached via email at cuicospirit@hotmail.com. His website is: www.ghostexcavation.com and he can be found on Facebook ("Ghost Excavations with John Sabol").

www.ingramcontent.com/pod-product-compliance
Lightning Source LLC
Chambersburg PA
CBHW050517160726
48003CB00001B/346